# Embracing Divine Wisdom in Distressing Times

## Wisdom Brings Peace to the Unexpected Chaos of Life

### Wanda Anderson

Delights of Truth

Published by Delights of Truth (delightsoftruth.com)
ISBN 979-8-9990248-0-0

eBook ISBN 979-8-999-0248-1-7

Cover Design by Joshua C. Anderson

Edited by Carrie Turner (Carrie Turner: Writing & Editing Services; www.carriebturner.com)

Author Photo by Melody Ochterbeck (www.instagram.com/melodyoch)

# CONTENTS

# DEDICATION

This book is dedicated to every mom (and dad) who seek wisdom from above when praying for their grown children who are going through personal struggles in life. Prayer changes our own perspective from what we desire for our children, to what the Lord God desires for them. I also dedicate this book to my family, especially to our son, Jeremy, who has graciously granted me the honor of sharing his part of my story. His experience of turmoil was the catalyst that pushed me to seek wisdom from God in a way I hadn't had to before. I am proud of the man you have become. In praying for you, I grew immensely in my understanding of God's ways while trusting Him to lead you into what He has planned for you.

# EMBRACING DIVINE WISDOM IN DISTRESSING TIMES

## WISDOM BRINGS PEACE TO THE UNEXPECTED CHAOS OF LIFE

# INTRODUCTION

When my husband and I got married, he was living in Kuwait. That meant I was adjusting not only to being a wife at the age of twenty-nine but also to a country I'd never lived in before. I tried to prepare myself for a new country and culture ahead of time, but I would still face challenges needing to be handled wisely. Learning to get around by car was one of these challenges—I couldn't read Arabic, and road signs were nearly non-existent. I instead relied on visuals along the route to get to a destination. I remember one specific day when I thought I had my directions well in hand, but then things went awry. Where was that abandoned car that always told me where to turn? I'd driven far enough that nothing looked familiar. Suddenly, I realized I was lost in a foreign country as a newlywed woman all on my own to either find my way to my destination or back to our apartment.

Wisdom was certainly needed at this point. We often describe wisdom with words such as understanding, common sense, good judgment, skillfulness, shrewdness, or just making good decisions. All these meanings are incorporated in the word *wisdom*. While growing up, we learn to make good decisions through observation, teaching, and experience. However, our experience falls short when we fail to rightly apply what we've learned.

My husband had patiently attempted to show me my route to and from the ladies Bible study I would be teaching at the next day. Because I've always been more of a hands-on learner, observation alone failed me since he was the driver while I had been the passenger. I had thought I would remember, yet there I was, lost with no way to contact him (this was before cell phones). There was nothing ahead of me but sand.

"Lord, I need your wisdom to get home because there's no way I know how to get to the villa I'm heading to. Please show me the way home," I had prayed.

Kuwait is a small country with ring-roads. A thought came to me—if I headed off the road and into the nearest neighborhood, I would find a ring-road that would lead me to the coastline and then to my home. I put that thought into action. Once I saw the Kuwait Towers in front of me, I relaxed. I knew the way to our apartment from that point on. My very relieved husband, who had received a phone call asking where I was, greeted me at the door with a hug. While I hugged my husband back, I silently gave thanks to the Lord for His download of simple wisdom that was easily put into practical action. It was a welcome relief to be back home.

Proverbs 2:2-3 encourages us to seek wisdom as though it were silver, a buried treasure to be discovered. We receive this treasure of wisdom by listening to God's Word spoken to us either by those who know it well or by reading the scriptures which instruct us. Then, we can focus our hearts on understanding how receiving wisdom works by applying it in our lives. This same proverb explains that when wisdom enters your heart, it is accompanied by knowledge which is pleasant to your soul. Wisdom then produces within you a discretion to guard and protect you (Proverbs 2:10-11). That's an awesome result produced within our lives just from seeking and pursuing wisdom.

In this book, we will investigate this process of finding the hidden treasure called *wisdom*. There is a beginning point called the "fear of the Lord" that we'll also explore. Throughout the course of our lives, we learn little by little as wisdom shines its light of truth. It brings us to a place of protection and discretion as we submit to divine strategy.

The process of treasuring God's Word, deeply embedding it into our hearts, is an important step to attaining wisdom. What does that look like and how do we do that? I have experienced decades of walking with Jesus, learning from Him, and asking for wisdom. I've seen how wisdom has helped me avoid painful situations, relieve my distress, and yield success. Throughout these pages, I hope to give you the insights I have acquired by asking and then trusting the Lord to share His wisdom with me. Wisdom increases as a person lives, both in the natural world and in wisdom from above. Understanding also increases as our lives advance. (Job 12:12).

I'm thankful for the Lord Jesus who took me by the hand and the heart to lead me to my Father God, who created me. His goodness knows no bounds. I have found Him to be all-wise, full of understanding—especially when I'm lacking in any given moment—and thoroughly committed to assisting me in every step of life's journey. I'm thankful for the Holy Spirit who walks beside me to fill me with His power to hear, see, and understand what the Word of God speaks of. I'm thankful for God's written Word that is ever fresh and new with revelation, broader understanding, and encouragement that leaps off the Bible's pages into the need of my heart and soul. I've been reading it now for nearly seventy years. Of course, my parents read it to me daily before I could read it for myself. My entire life has literally been steeped in the pages of God's written Word.

Jeremiah the prophet was so right when he penned the words about God's faithful mercies and compassions being renewed daily. God's faithfulness is so very great. He pours out His goodness to each person who looks to Him for help and counsel (Lamentations 3:22-23). When we seek and pursue wisdom, we are seeking and pursuing God. To know Him is to walk in His ways while pursuing His heart.

Come with me as we pursue wisdom together. If you're ready for this adventure, then ask expectantly for wisdom. The Lord has promised to share His infinite wealth of wisdom with you as you draw closer to Him. Let's get started!

# The Need for Wisdom

"For the Lord gives wisdom: out of his mouth comes knowledge and understanding." – Proverbs 2:6 [NEW KING JAMES TRANSLATION]

*Wow! This is an incredible adventure!* I thought as we soared through the sky. *The sky is so blue; there's so many breathtaking views! We're soaring vertically, straight up, into the heavens. Amazing!* Then the view changed, as I knew it would. The Cessna 150 shuddered slightly, the engine stalling as it was supposed to, just before the airplane turned earthward. At the same time the airplane began to spin round and round. I was enjoying the adventure. As my view spiraled, I totally trusted the pilot to pull the airplane out of its spin. That's when I heard the private pilot instructor beside me say, "I know you've done this practice before in the passenger seat. But today, *you* are the pilot. Pull this airplane out of its spin now!"

Oh yes! I was the pilot in charge. I needed to focus on the instrument panel in front of me, not on the downward curving view outside the window. I needed to pull us out of the spin and not expect the instructor to take over for me. That's why we were in the air, to allow me time to practice under his supervision.

Seeking wisdom by pursuing God is similar. You often learn through study and observation, whether through instruction or elsewhere; you may uncover wonders upon wonders of godly wisdom from the examples shared by teachers of the Bible you listen to. But until you apply that knowledge and make it work for you; it won't become a story or testimony of your life. The instrument panel of the airplane I was flying represents, to me, how both natural wisdom and wisdom from above guides us to apply what we have learned properly. By learning from God's Word, and then appropriately applying the principles of wise living I can navigate the circumstances I find myself in. When we ask Father God for wisdom, He gives us an understanding of how to apply the principles found in scripture. It will require you to focus on what is necessary instead of distractions vying for your attention.

In reference to the above analogy, I safely pulled the Cessna 150 out of its spin. Wisdom demanded that I pay attention to the instrument panel in front of me rather than what surrounded me. This is true in any life situation. Wisdom guides us to safety when we pay attention to what must be said or done rather than fixating on the details of the circumstances distracting us from appropriate action. Scripture is much like that instrument panel. Wisdom, on the other hand, is knowing both how each instrument works and which to prioritize and pay attention to at any given moment.

Dictionaries define wisdom as common sense. Your commonsense kicks in when needed, such as when you've lost your way. You need to avoid panic to navigate sensibly to the destination. Commonsense comes from good judgment. Judging a situation clearly will provide you with a wise outlook, plan, or course of action. Being physically lost would require you to stop to look at a map or GPS, take stock of your surroundings, and then trust the map or GPS to get you on the right course.

Wisdom is the ability to discern or judge what is true, right, or lasting. It gives us insight into things that are unknown. All of us develop natural wisdom as we learn from life experiences—by trial and error—as well as through instruction and observation. We all have common sense to greater or lesser degrees. Both natural and godly wisdom develop this way. Practical wisdom is what we live by, survive by, and make decisions by.

There are times when I've needed wisdom that isn't just practical but divine. Divine wisdom taps into God's strategic ability to see the end from the beginning and everything in between. His is a higher wisdom. In the Bible, James said: "But the wisdom that is from above is first pure, then peaceable, gentle, willing to yield, full of mercy and good fruits, without partiality and without hypocrisy" (James 3:17 [NKJ]). This is a very different definition than what we find in a dictionary. This means there are two kinds of wisdom: a natural wisdom; and a wisdom "from above," or wisdom from God who created everything. We need both.

Natural wisdom serves us well until we encounter a situation requiring something better. That's when we realize we need God's wisdom to safely navigate this situation. God's wisdom is *pure*, or holy, in its essence. It is blameless, and without any defects. It promotes peace of heart, mind, and soul not only to the person applying God's wisdom, but to others who are recipients of its effect.

I often turn to scripture to see what counsel can be gleaned from its pages. People who have sought the Lord for wisdom generations ago come to life right before my eyes. Solomon, a man who asked God for wisdom when stepping into his father's shoes as ruler of Israel, is one of these people. Of course, I don't rule a nation, but I find making household decisions often requires wisdom from above.

King Solomon is described in scripture as the wisest of all men in his day, though he didn't start out that way. He asked God for wisdom and, because he asked, Father God gave him such a wealth of wisdom that rumor of it spread all the way to the Queen of Sheba. She traveled to Israel to observe and talk with him, verifying whether what she had heard of him was true. Yet as much wisdom as Solomon received from God, his falls short of the wisdom that Jesus, God's Son, is known for. Jesus, when comparing King Solomon's wisdom with the wisdom of God, stated that "greater wisdom is here" (Matthew 12:42 [NKJ]). What does that mean?

King Solomon gained natural wisdom because he was well-educated, having studied widely all manners of subjects. He was intelligent enough to retain and apply what he'd learned. He was skillful in matters of war and in the administration of the land he ruled, shrewd in what he set himself to learn and discover, and in his moral attitudes, and ethics. This is not to say he never failed to be wise from time to time, but for the most part, he learned that his natural wisdom needed to be overlayed by wisdom from above. This distinction built his reputation of wisdom, sending it beyond his kingdom to the ears of other rulers.

Yet, in that record of Solomon's deep wisdom, scripture does not compare it to the wisdom of Jesus. Why? Because the wisdom Jesus walked in as the Son of God is far superior to any wisdom found on Earth. He continually exercised wisdom from above rather than only natural wisdom gleaned through life experiences. His depth of understanding often astounded those around Him.

Since Jesus's wisdom is greater than Solomon's, in its perfection and application, how do we access it? Where do we get this wisdom from above defined as pure, peaceable, patient, willing to yield, full of mercy, full of good fruit, without either partiality, or hypocrisy (James 3:17 [NKJV])? Again, scripture gives us the answer by stating that we must ask God for it. Ask for wisdom and He will pour it out in abundance. Can it possibly be just that simple? Whenever I've asked for wisdom from above, I then act on what is given to me, whether it be from a thought or vision in my mind. I encourage you to ask Him today for the wisdom you need now. Then grab hold of whatever thought He puts into your mind, act on it, and see what He does with your obedience and trust in Him.

# NATURAL VS DIVINE WISDOM

"With Him are wisdom and strength, He has counsel and understanding." –Job 12:13 [NEW KING JAMES VERSION]

It all began with a simple phone call. After speaking briefly, my son hung up the phone and informed me of an appointment he'd made to meet with a recruiter to discuss joining the Marine Corp. My motherly heart lurched. I asked my son how this came about. Recruiters were visiting the high school seeking volunteers to enlist. They appealed to Jeremy, hence the phone call. That moment became the first step of a walk of faith requiring me to seek wisdom from my heavenly Father.

In the days following that phone call, I tried to talk my son into rethinking his decision to join the Marines. Since he was not yet eighteen, they required a signature from me and my husband to give Jeremy permission to join. My husband assured me this was the right thing to do—to give our permission rather than make him wait. A full year would go by as Jeremy finished his final year of high school.

One day, I was in prayer over the turmoil in my heart when the Lord gave me a vision: my son was laid out peacefully in a casket. The Lord gently asked, "Will you withhold your son from Me?" My heart wanted to cry out, "Yes, I will withhold him!" But instead, I broke into tears as my spirit quietly responded, "No, Lord, You gave him to me in the first place. I place him back into Your loving hands." My signature was a sign of trusting the Lord to fulfill His plan and purpose in the life of our son.

Everyone has some degree of wisdom. We need wisdom in business, in relationships, and in whatever life situation we need to navigate. Jesus said that people of this world are wiser in dealing with their contemporaries than those He revealed His light to (Luke 16:8). That's a sad comparison. Those who follow Jesus should be learning how to be wiser in all areas of living. After all, we have a relationship with the very person scripture says *is* wisdom—Jesus. His wisdom should be on display to those around us throughout our lives. In the situation with my son, I was realizing just how much I needed His wisdom in calming my fears, hearing His voice, and trusting His counsel.

Jesus illustrated natural wisdom by telling a story about a financial businessman in Luke 16:1-13. The businessman's employer asked for an account of his administration once he had heard of his misappropriation of company funds. This financial manager schemed to escape the consequences of theft by reducing the debt of the company's clients. In doing so, he ingratiated himself to them while presumably rectifying the misappropriated funds which reaccumulated for deposit back into the company's bank account. Jesus did not tell the end of this story, but you can imagine a few outcomes for yourself. The wisdom this manager displayed may have saved him from being fired or worse, but it is different in the way wisdom from heaven would work. This man's wisdom involved manipulation combined with deception to serve himself best. His motive was selfish. Wisdom from God never includes those kinds of motivations!

Natural wisdom is driven by the motivations of our hearts, often based on the needs we face plus our desired outcome. This manager needed to replace the funds he had stolen. The motivation of his heart was to hide the wrongdoing that got him into that situation in the first place. It certainly didn't come from a place of blamelessness, so it wasn't pure, though it was a shrewd maneuver that mainly benefited himself. Scripture states that if we are motivated by bitter envy and self-seeking, then we make our boast by lying rather than being truthful (James 3:14-16). That kind of wisdom does not come from above. It is earth-bound, natural in its origin, and even demonic in nature. Where there is jealousy and selfishness, there is disorder and evil in every act.

The story of Joseph is a contrasting example of wisdom that more appropriately demonstrates godly wisdom (Genesis 37, 39-42, 45-50). Joseph suffered years of misunderstanding, mistreatment, and abuse from his family and others. In fact, one false accusation resulted in a prison sentence. Joseph could have sat with a victim's mentality, nursing his wounded soul from that point forward. He even could have thought to retaliate and justify himself. Instead, he sought the Lord and applied himself to bring order and peace to his inmates. It wasn't long before the results of his actions got the warden's attention. He recognized that Joseph's wisdom contributed to peaceful prison conditions. So, Joseph was made an overseer of the cells. He listened to the concerns of his fellow prisoners then spoke God's counsel, not his own. He kept his motivation pure. He sincerely wanted to help others, not just himself.

Joseph's purity of wisdom eventually reached the ear of the Pharoah of Egypt. Pharoah was so impressed that he promoted Joseph from prisoner to Administrator over every region under his rule. That was the result of purity of wisdom operating in Joseph's life that came directly from Almighty God.

Joseph believed God knew all about the abuses of life he encountered. Joseph trusted God to direct his responses in every situation. He was peaceable in navigating difficulties with people wherever he found himself. Godly wisdom helped Joseph understand that God intended to redeem all he had been through. This redemption came about through reconciliation with his brothers who were riddled with guilt over mistreating him years earlier. With God's wisdom, Joseph was able to let go of any attitude that could have led him into retribution. Instead, he grabbed hold of God's plan to restore, redeem, and reconcile with his family through an attitude of love. Joseph's story ended happily with full reconciliation in his family, and he was honored.

It reminds me, again, of this passage from James 3:17-18 [NKJV]:

"But the wisdom that is from above is first pure, then peaceable, gentle, willing to yield, full of mercy and good fruits, without partiality, and without hypocrisy. Now the fruit of righteousness is sown in peace by those who make peace."

Wisdom from above is "pure," meaning holy. There's no hidden motivation or purpose other than doing what is best for anyone involved. Wisdom comes from the heart of Father God who has no shifting purposes within Himself. Love is the motivating force of the wisdom He pours into our hearts and minds. With it, we can bring peace to volatile situations and find a way that mercifully accommodates those involved. This godly wisdom is pure, clean, and modest in the way it operates, bringing true justice without partiality or hypocrisy. It certainly had to be worked into my own heart. That is why the Lord gave me the vision of my son as He did, followed by the question He asked. His questions probe the heart and purge it from selfish motivations.

Another good example of wisdom in demonstration is found yet again in the story of King Solomon. He had to make a judgment when two women both claimed to be the mother of the same child (1 Kings 3:16-28). His decision to divide the child in half so each woman would have half the child may not make sense to us at first. In fact, we may even think it sounds ludicrously cruel. Yet that judgment ultimately revealed the child's true mother as King Solomon intended. She was the one who immediately sought to preserve the child's life by relinquishing her claim to him. She wanted to preserve her child's life, while the woman falsely claiming to be his mother agreed to have the child killed. The other woman's falsehood was thus exposed and dealt with appropriately. As news of this event spread, the entire nation revered the king because they saw that the wisdom of God was in him. His understanding brought out the truth and others recognized God's wisdom. In this story, God's wisdom may have sounded harsh, but it successfully exposed a lie, doing no harm in the end.

Just as Solomon applied wisdom from above to discover the rightful mother, the Lord's heart-probing question helped me realize that, even though I was Jeremy's mom, he ultimately belonged to the God who created and loved him more than I could.

All of us will eventually need to trust God with the lives of our children. He has a multitude of ways to interact with their lives for their benefit—ways we as parents never could. Have you committed your children to the Lord? If not, why not? Do you trust His wisdom to safely bring them through whatever they are facing? I encourage you to trust the Lord to give you wisdom as well as the courage to trust His counsel, even if it doesn't make sense yet. He is all-wise and faithful.

# Ask for Wisdom

"If any of you lack wisdom, let him ask of God, who gives to all liberally and without reproach, and it will be given to him." –James 1:5 [NEW KING JAMES VERSION]

June 14, 2004. Jeremy's departure date for boot camp had a day and time. As a last outing the weekend before he was to ship out, Jeremy went on a camping trip with friends. He had an accident that caused a gash to the heel of his hand and wrist. This injury put off his departure for another two weeks.

It was then that Jeremy told me he felt the Lord had spoken to him: "Two delays in becoming a Marine will be the sign that I would not become a Marine." He had talked with Marine officers about changing his mind, but they informed him it was not allowed while the USA had troops in Iraq under war conditions. Opting not to report to boot camp would mean immediate arrest as a deserter.

That led me to begin asking the Lord for wisdom. I asked to see His plans for Jeremy become reality. Through that process, He helped me deal with my own feelings and misgivings about Jeremy's upcoming departure. I sensed the Lord wanted to redirect him, but I also felt a deep sense of powerlessness over the whole situation. I acknowledged that God was in control, so I turned to Him for help in my time of need.

Amid my emotional turmoil, I was aware that God, in His infinite wisdom, knew what was needed in this very challenging situation with my son. He is the source of wisdom from above and we simply need to ask Him for the wisdom we need at any time. What is His response to us when we ask for wisdom? He gives us a download of His wisdom in abundant measures—more than we could imagine.

I needed God's wisdom. I truly believed that if I asked Him for wisdom to navigate my circumstances, He would give it to me liberally and without rebuking. Through His wisdom, I hoped to gain an ability to apply knowledge, experience, understanding, common sense, and insight to a very unsettling time.

Job's definition of wisdom—"The fear of the Lord, that is wisdom; and to depart from evil is understanding—" brought great comfort to my conflicted heart (Job 28:28 [NKJV]). The fear of the Lord didn't mean that I was to be *afraid* of God but to have a reverential awe of His power, majesty, love, and greatness. This enabled me to trust His counsel in the days that followed.

Christ Jesus is, for us, wisdom who came from God. He brings to us His righteousness, sanctification, and redemption (1 Corinthians 1:30). God our Father, through Jesus, "gives us the spirit of wisdom and revelation in the knowledge of Him" (Ephesians 1:17 [NKJV]). When we ask for wisdom from above, He teaches us in a multitude of ways the authority of God that we have access to, not only for defeating the principalities and powers of the world, but as a godly course of action that directs our behavior (Ephesians 3:10-11). It bears repeating that James described God's wisdom as pure. It has no selfish motivation attached to it. God's wisdom is clean and innocent in its application. It is peaceable, always seeking out a peaceful outcome for everyone. God's wisdom is gentle and patient. We show our respect and trust in God when we simply ask for wisdom. His wisdom is full of mercy because God is compassionate. Therefore, His wisdom is grounded in compassion. God's wisdom is full of good fruits, meaning beneficial actions that help heal souls. It is without partiality and without hypocrisy (James 3:17). There is no selfish agenda in God's wisd om.

We are to grow in wisdom throughout our lives. This was the challenge I was facing. Was I willing to ask for and grow in godly wisdom while also learning to act on it? Jeremy's situation required me to continually ask for, search out, and acquire God's wisdom daily. This is true for all of us. When we acquire wisdom, we must then learn to rightly apply it. The starting point, the most important step, is to ask and keep on asking. We will grow more skillful in acting upon the wisdom we receive, and our ability will become more reliable over time. I was willing to ask. Equally important, I was willing to act on what the Lord said. I encourage you to ask the Lord for the wisdom that you need to walk in today. Then, confidently do what He says.

When asking for wisdom, it is important to ask from a humble heart and the desire to spend time with our Creator. We approach Him through our Savior Jesus. Spending time with Him in prayer and quietness opens our hearts to receive wisdom and authority from Him. He grows our understanding of who He is and what His ways are. We ask with expectancy, and we keep on asking until we receive it.

There will be times when we don't receive His wisdom immediately simply because our hearts and souls are too distracted by what we're going through. Those distractions become blinders over our eyes and a plug in our ears. Yet He is faithful to us. He will ensure that, at a moment when we're free from distractions, we'll step out to do what He has instructed, like Peter did in scripture. Peter stepped out of the boat he was in, into the water at Jesus' invitation "come" when he and his friends were at sea amid a raging storm. Peter obeyed Jesus' call to step out of the wind-battered boat, but then he became distracted by the storm. That distraction, coupled with fear, caused him to sink into the waves. If only he had kept his eyes on Jesus! And yet, despite his lack of faith, Jesus immediately grabbed hold of him. He helped Peter continue walking on the water. Jesus does the same for us! He brings awareness to His presence as He grabs hold of us, helping us use His wisdom—wisdom that overcomes our natural settings.

Apart from the Lord Jesus, we cannot walk in divine wisdom. As we grow in the knowledge of the Lord and His ways, the Holy Spirit will teach us how to apply that knowledge. Walking wisely demonstrates the power of God working within and through us in love.

We should ask Him for wisdom for the day. Ask for understanding and help to apply the knowledge we already have. Ask God to help us grab hold of His inexhaustibly vast supply of wisdom (Romans 11:33).

Our Father God, the creator of everything in the universe, knew all that was needed prior to creating mankind. He still has that fore-knowledge. He makes His all-knowing wisdom available to us through our Lord Jesus Christ. When we ask for wisdom and God pours it into us, we then need the understanding to apply it to our hearts (Proverbs 2:2). The Lord becomes our shield of protection as our soul discovers the pleasantness of the knowledge of God and His ways (Proverbs 2:7, 10).

As I asked the Lord for wisdom, His words became a shield to my heart and soul, guarding me from ungrounded fears. His peace flowed into me enabling me to have confidence that He was in the unseen details of my son's life—whether I fully understood or not. You will benefit from God's wisdom in unexpected ways, just as I did. He will quickly grab hold of you whenever you're feeling overwhelmed. He will bring back stability and will give you the ability to trust in what He has said––just as He did with Peter, and just as He did with me.

# WISDOM LEADS TO UNDERSTANDING

"Wisdom is the principal thing; therefore, get wisdom. And in all your getting, get understanding." –Proverbs 4:7 [NEW KING JAMES VERSION]

It was June 21, 2004, at 3:30 a.m. Our son walked out the front door for a drive to the airport and a flight that would take him 2,000 miles away for Marine Basic Training. Since a second delay had not occurred, Jeremy embraced the perspective of this journey being a huge step into adulthood, making life-directing decisions that he alone was responsible for. My heart broke to see him leave.

I spent the next three days praying for him and listened daily for the phone to ring. It did, many times, though none of the rings meant our son was on the other end.

Then, the day he called finally came! He was feeling extremely homesick by the time he was allowed to call home. But because the static on the line was so bad, I didn't recognize his voice. I hung up on him with the words, "Sir, can you call back, please? I can't clearly hear anything said because of static." That left him in tears. A second call was not permitted even when the first one was unsuccessful.

He wrote to us about it not long after, explaining the situation. How it broke my heart to read those words in his letter. Bursting into tears, I ran to the Lord for comfort. I prayed a lot because the vision I had had of our son dead in a coffin was still so strong. My separation from him was hard because of it. Still, the Lord's grace would bring peace to my aching heart again and again while I adjusted to Jeremy being away from home. His many letters helped, too.

During training, as Jeremy told us later, the Lord was also speaking to him. "You will not see combat." More specifically, He told him, "You will not learn to shoot a weapon. You will be a man of peace, not a man of war."

At home, I was often on my face on the bedroom floor, weeping before the Lord, pleading with Him to be merciful to our son and separate him from the Marine Corps. And should He ultimately choose it, to give me the grace to handle Jeremy's death.

Yet, I also reminded the Lord of His compassion for the mother in Luke 7:12-15 when her son had died. Out of compassion, He raised her son from the dead and presented him back to her. God did it for her; He could do it for me.

Before long, the phone rang again. The Lord was using that simple little invention of man so evidently in my life as a steppingstone to seeking His wisdom. It began ringing at 11:30 in the evening. Having already fallen asleep, my husband answered with a sleepy "hello." Instantly, he was sitting up in bed asking questions.

"How long have you been in the hospital?" I heard my husband ask from the other side of the bed. "What did the doctor say? How do you feel now?"

I was immediately alert and moved closer to my husband's side to discover what had happened. Jeremy had suffered a heat stroke and nearly died. His only prayer request was, "Dad, Mom, pray for the Lord to give me many opportunities to share the gospel with as many as I can for as long as I can."

As my husband hung up the phone, we began to pray. The Lord gave me another vision. This time it was of a huge cloud-like hand surrounding a tiny little figure of a man—our son, Jeremy. Slowly, that hand began to scoop our son right out of the Marines. This second vision brought peace to my heart and helped me rest my eyes after that phone call. It also began a time of seeking wisdom through pursuing God's heart and counsel. My question to the Lord was, "How does Your plan for our son's life overrule the plans of the US Marine Corps? How does Your wisdom work in this situation?"

The next two months were a roller-coaster ride of emotion. The only stability of mind and heart came from the Lord Jesus speaking specific scriptures to me, teaching me to hold tightly to Him no matter how confusing the circumstances. His words combatted against well-meant words spoken to me by friends. Their words of intended encouragement often had the opposite effect.

"Let your son go."

"Cut those apron-strings and let him be a man."

Jesus kept my emotions afloat when fellow believers prayed for Jeremy to be miraculously healed and sent back into Basic Training to complete what he'd started. They didn't believe that I heard the Lord correctly, nor that Jeremy had heard Him correctly. Being a Marine was not a bad career choice after all. Psalm 33 came alive to me:

"Rejoice in the Lord, O you righteous! For praise from the upright is beautiful...For the word of the Lord is right, and all His work is done in truth. He loves righteousness and justice; the earth is full of the goodness of the Lord...For He spoke, and it was done; He commanded, and it stood fast. The Lord brings the counsel of the nations to nothing; He makes the plans of the peoples of no effect. The counsel of the Lord stands forever, the plans of His heart to all generations...The Lord looks from heaven; He sees all the sons of men. From the place of His dwelling, He looks on all the inhabitants of the earth; He fashions their hearts individually" (Psalm 33:1, 4-5, 9-11, 13-15 [NKJV]).

Proverbs 22:3 [NKJV] tells us that "a prudent man foresees the evil, and hides himself; but the simple pass on, and are punished." This chapter in Proverbs compares the wise person and the unwise person in a variety of ways. In seeking wisdom, I intended to walk wisely and prudently. I also wanted to walk in the understanding that comes when the Lord gives us foresight into future things. Foresight is the ability to see ahead, knowing something in advance so one can plan wisely. A poor relative of foresight is a premonition, which is often experienced as a feeling of evil to come.

What is important about these two viewpoints? We as human beings often have premonitions—that gut-feeling that something is going to happen, something we want to avoid. These can be brought about by internal thoughts we're unaware of. My misunderstanding of that first vision of Jeremy in a coffin led me to misinterpret what the Lord's intention for him would be, producing a fear within me that had to be frequently wrestled with. God can give us foresight, or the wisdom to see ahead, because He knows all things—past, present, and future.

Foresight can occur naturally, as it is described in Luke 12:54-55, when Jesus talks about observing the sky and wind to determine whether a shower is coming or scorching heat. This type of foresight can be learned, and prepared for what foresight warns you of in advance. A well-known example is our ability to track hurricanes. God-inspired foresight is when He clues us into His foreknowledge. He shared His foresight with Jeremy with the words, "You will not learn to shoot a gun because you're a man of peace, not a man of war." He shared it with me in the vision of His hand scooping Jeremy out of the Marine Corps as well. It came with an understanding of how to pray effectively, according to the will of God.

He did this with Joseph, Jesus's earthly father, when Herod was plotting to kill all children aged under two. Joseph acted wisely upon that foreknowledge by departing with Mary and Jesus to a safer country. Natural foresight is good, but God's foresight is better in preparing and equipping us for the future ahead. Natural foresight is learned through the things we experience. God's foresight is much more accurate, and He makes it available to us. He couples it with His wisdom to help us avoid the schemes of the enemy, sidestep temptations, and walk in confidence with the Lord.

In seeking after wisdom, we seek after the heart of the God who created us. He pours His strength into our being, enabling us to stand up under pressure, see beyond what is troubling our minds, and express our trust in His ability. His wisdom helps us seek Him more persistently.

My first responsibility before the Lord, then, was to rejoice, with or without tears, depending on my day-to-day emotions. And so, I rejoiced! I encouraged myself in my God who is faithful and very near in the day of trouble. Then the Lord Jesus began to instruct me on how to turn those verses into prayers of power:

It is the Lord "who fashions each heart individually." – "A man's heart plans his way, but the Lord directs his steps" (Proverbs 16:9 [NKJV]).

By grabbing hold of that vision with the understanding of God's foreknowledge, I gained a new ability to pray into that foresight with confident trust in the Lord.

You can have that too. Trust what He shares with you in your time of prayer. Don't forget to rejoice before Him—even before the answer comes, even as you are getting to know Him. We rejoice because we've found Him. We rejoice because of His help. We rejoice because He sustains us and holds us up, so we don't fall. He fights for us, helping us to overcome every difficulty, to have victory over every distress and hardship. We rejoice because His words are truth and life, and they defeat the lies and tactics of the enemy of our souls, the devil.

# TREASURING GOD'S WORD

"My son, if you receive my words, and treasure my commands within you..." –Proverbs 2:1 [NEW KING JAMES VERSION]

It was by reading scripture and treasuring its insights that led me to learn how to fully worship the Lord. At the age of sixteen, I asked the Lord to teach me how to worship Him in a way that pleased Him. Immediately the words, "Read the Psalms and turn them into songs of praise," floated through my mind.

That's what I did. When I entered my bedroom to be alone with the Bible and the Lord's presence, I opened to the book of Psalms and began to read. I took the words that particularly grabbed my attention and turned them into songs of praise, songs coming from my heart to this creative God I wanted to know more personally. His presence filled my heart.

One evening, the door to my bedroom opened and, one by one, my parents and brothers entered to join me in prayer and worship. Why, I asked, did they do that? Was I singing too loud? They told me the presence of the Lord became so strong in the whole house that they had to stop what they were doing to join me. This led to frequent times of family worship and prayer. I grew to know the Lord by treasuring every word written in the Bible. I learned to apply its truths to the daily routines of my life. In addition, my family began to treasure those evening times of worship together. We experienced an overflow of our Father God's love for us as we treasured His Word in our lives.

Scripture encouraged me to seek after wisdom as one would seek after silver and gold (Proverbs 2:4). Silver and gold are precious metals. The purer the metal, the more costly it is. The Gold Rush demonstrates this belief of the value of silver and gold. People left their homes and families to seek a gold mine that would enrich them for years to come. Fortunately, we don't have to live in a harsh environment or search in caves or streams for wisdom. All we must do to find God's wisdom is go to the Father and ask Him for it. He will never withhold His wisdom from us.

When I began to place importance on spending a portion of every day reading the scriptures, I began to treasure every word, every command, and every encouragement the Bible spoke to my heart and mind. What began as a discipline became something I looked forward to. This is how treasuring God's Word begins to build and transform a person's life.

A treasure is something a person highly values. It is kept secure, guarded, and endears the heart. In fact, "where your treasure is, there your heart will be also," (Matthew 6:21). Jesus says that people speak out of what they have treasured or stored up in their hearts (Matthew 12:35). If we've stored up good things, it comes through our words and actions. Those words and actions define our character. Jesus is the Word, and life is found in Him through hearing the word (John 1:1; 5:24). The more we know of Jesus through the written Word, the more quickly scripture comes to mind at any given time, and the more it guides us in relationships, business, and times of difficulty. It reveals who God is as well as how He interacts with us.

Scripture tells us that God's Word is truth (Psalm 119:160; John 17:17). When scripture begins to find its place inside of you, it begins to defeat our negative self-talk, softens our attitudes, corrects our perceptions, and heals our relationships. Because I began to treasure God's Word daily by reading and meditating on it, I found my attitudes and perceptions changing to align with what scripture says. Also, my relationships began to take on a new-found dynamic of God's love enabling me to forgive quickly any slight or offense by others, thereby protecting my heart. The Word of God enlightened my understanding of situations and grew my trust in the Lord. The Lord desires for truth to reside in the internal depths of our being (Psalm 51:6). It's in the depth of our soul, soaking in God's Word, that wisdom grows, developing into maturity. We allow the Word to become a part of us through reading it many times, memorizing it, and putting it into practice.

For me, it meant a daily practice of taking my fears to the Lord to release them into His capable hands. It made sense because He was the only one who could deliver me. As Psalm 34:4 [NKJV] says: "I sought the Lord, and He heard me, and delivered me from all my fears." I had to learn to seek Him frequently. That practice affected my outlook because spending time with God changes us.

Spending time daily in the scriptures grows our relationship with the author of them: God. To treasure God's Word is to treasure time with God in all His capacities—as Father, Son, and Holy Spirit.

As you receive His written word into your inner being, take time to ponder it throughout the day, just like how a child might slip a treasure into his pocket to secretly carry with him wherever he goes. Write out a verse or passage that leaps off the page so you can re-read it wherever you happen to be. Memorize it. You will begin to sense a change deep within you. You will start to anticipate seeing Jesus, the Word, alive and working in your relationships and activities. The Word will come into your mind, giving you help in the moments of your day when you really need God's wisdom. This leads to a sensitivity to the ways and words of God throughout your day. You will find yourself leaning into the Word of God, listening for His voice to speak to you from the scriptures.

Proverbs 2:2 [NKJV] counsels you to "incline your ear to wisdom and apply your heart to understanding." I love that the Hebrew word for incline simply means to "prick up the ears." This brings to my mind our dog when we say a word that interests him. He immediately tilts his head and perks up his ears to intently listen to my voice. He observes what I am saying with my voice and body language. We do similarly with the Word of God. When a passage in scripture leaps off the page, it grabs the attention of both our hearts and ears as we observe and listen to what the Lord is saying to us. Hearing starts the process of developing an ear for His voice. We learn to distinguish the voice of the Lord God from our own voice by knowing what He says in scripture. The power of observation comes through when we see the context surrounding the verses that grabbed our attention—just as my dog listens intently to me while observing my actions to know my intention. Am I speaking and grabbing his leash? That means, to him, we will go for a walk. In the same way, our hearts become attuned to the Lord by treasuring His precious Word and studying why those words grabbed our attention. His Word then motivates us to do what He says.

Cherishing God's Word will ignite a heart of worship in us. Our vocabulary for expressing our thoughts, emotions, and needs to the God who created us will grow. Treasuring the scriptures brings us closer to the author of those very words, Jesus, our Savior, and Redeemer. Jesus came into this world to dwell among mankind as one of us, for the express purpose of being a living example to humanity. He has returned to His place as King in eternity, yet His presence still infuses us with grace and truth when we read His words of life.

Treasuring God's Word allows it to influence us in every area of life when we stretch out to grab hold of it until it becomes a part of who we are. We ask Him for wisdom appropriate for every given opportunity. Because we honor the Word, our thoughts begin to reflect healthier patterns, which in turn affect our decisions and interactions with others. Personally, I've become more patient, more compassionate, and humbler, hopefully, because of what I've read in the scriptures. Delighting in God's Word has created within me a fresh desire to please Him in ways that are different from before.

Those weeks I spent going into my bedroom to read the scriptures became a daily habit lasting through the decades. The spontaneous worship and prayer meetings within my family home have become precious testimonies of discovering who God is. They are memories that remain and encourage me even today. From those times spent in the Word, I came to understand who God created me to be, as well as what direction my life would take. I let His Word pour into my soul and heart to refresh me, wash me, correct any misunderstanding or error, and to let His wisdom fill me with courage. This is what treasuring the Word of God brings into our lives!

What about you? Do you treasure God's Word daily? If not—or if only sometimes—then ask Him to help you treasure Him and His Word today! He loves to answer that request!

There's an endless supply of wisdom in the scriptures. As you seek to know God better from reading the Bible, you will find yourself adopting the ways of God, His plans, and purposes for your life. His Word will teach you how to live and will influence every area of your life daily. Along with the knowledge of God, knowing the scriptures brings an understanding that enables you to rightly apply them to specific circumstances. Scripture teaches you to overcome difficulties and distractions as you set your mind on the God who created this world that He's placed you in.

# POSITIONED TO HEAR THE LORD

"The fear of the Lord is the beginning of wisdom; a good understanding have all those who do His commandments. His praise endures forever." –Psalm 111:10 [NEW KING JAMES VERSION]

I well remember agonizing over some of the actions of one of our teen sons, when suddenly, I had a vision that seemed so real. In the vision our newly purchased, second-hand car got demolished. Though the "how" was not apparent in the vision, it drove me to pray against this happening because I knew our son would be driving it.

After praying intently over this vision, with the things I'd learned about rebuking the attacks of the enemy, I finally grew quiet. I distinctly heard the Lord ask, "Are you finished? Do you want to hear why I gave you that vision?" That got my attention! As I asked the Lord for clarity, He assured me that the vision would become reality. The car would indeed be demolished. However, His purpose in allowing this was to give me a touchpoint of His mercy and grace to the son driving it. He also assured me our son would not be hurt nor would anyone else in that car with him.

The following day, I headed out to pick our middle son up from school. When coming to the T-intersection, I saw our car in a ditch. A tree was on top of it completely crushing the roof. The front doors on both sides were open, the engine running, the radio playing, and a polic e officer was walking around the car. I pulled over to ask him where my son was. He asked, "is this your car, ma'am?" Of course, it was. My son and his friend were perfectly fine; only the car was demolished.

Because scripture encourages us to set our hearts and souls on seeking the Lord, this is what I determined to do (1 Chronicles 22:19). Though I initially acted on my own interpretation of the vision, which caused me to pray as I did, the Lord's questioning of me made me realize I should have responded with wisdom, seeking to hear His purpose for the vision and its true meaning.

Seeking the Lord, for me, can mean spending time reading the Bible along with time pouring out my soul's concerns and desires to Him. Also, time spent worshipping Him helps clear my soul of any distracting thoughts. Most importantly, however, is the time spent quietly listening for His voice. His voice usually sounds like my own voice, though His words are not necessarily words I might use when speaking to myself. His voice leaves the impression upon my soul to pay attention. When I have asked the Lord for His wise counsel, He has at times spoken immediately because I was ready to hear. At other times, He would speak through a dream in the night that gave me clarity of what I should say or do as I awaken thinking of that dream. Still, other times He has spoken to me through the scriptures I read by giving a newfound understanding of them. Often, He delays until

I'm ready to hear, then speaks as I go about the things I need to get done in my day.

To seek after wisdom is to position ourselves to hear the Lord. This requires that we focus our minds on eternal truths over the facts of the situation we face, such as the Lord's purpose for that vision I had of our car (Colossians 3:1-2). We seek God-answers, not human-answers, for solutions. We seek His thoughts, guidance, and purpose for the situations we find ourselves in. God is always willing to give wise counsel and foresight when He speaks to us. Therefore, we strive to enter into agreement with His counsel by applying His Word to our lives when He speaks. We especially want to act on what we hear Him say to our hearts.

In times of stress or crisis, our need causes us to seek the Lord in all His of capacities—

as the Father of all creation who knows the end from the beginning; the Son who Redeems our lives, reconciles us to the Father, and delivers us from all trouble, snares, and temptations; and the Holy Spirit who gives us boldness to believe, hear, and obey God's voice with bold confidence. Afterall, our unwanted difficulties are common to mankind. But God promises to be faithful to us. He promises to provide a way to navigate our circumstances, whether we view them wrongly or desire to avoid them. And He promises to pour His grace, stability, and ability into us as a testimony confirming His goodness (1 Corinthians 10:13).

What does hearing God's voice look like daily? Jesus, our prime example, clearly laid out His own need to do this in the Gospel of John when He stated that He didn't seek His own will, but the will of His Father. He told His disciples that the words He spoke were not His own, but the words He heard His Father speak, and the things He did were what He saw His Father do (John 5:30, 14:20). Jesus often withdrew from the busyness of life to spend time with His Father in prayer. After that time of prayer, He then would re-engage with people, sharing what He had received from His Father. The same needs to be true of us. It certainly needed to be true in my life, especially after receiving that disturbing vision from the Lord about our car!

All of us are acquainted with the distress and trouble that wear on the soul. We need the Lord to bolster us with the courage and the wisdom only He can give. Once we receive the Lord's wise counsel, all we need to do is to act on what He has spoken of. Seeking God's counsel and wisdom in practical ways can look like many different things: seeking His voice in scripture, hearing His voice in a thought that comes to mind, experiencing a dream or vision, or audibly hearing His voice. When we hear Him, we should do what we've heard, just as Jesus did. If we lack understanding, we need to go back to Him for clarity. To hear the Lord's counsel may require that we wait upon Him until we are ready to hear. The process of waiting on Him looks like setting our heart and mind upon Him, allowing distractions to depart from us, and settling ourselves to listen. This is exactly what I needed to do to get past my own misunderstanding of the vision I'd received. I needed His wise perspective and His explanation of the vision so that I could speak and do what He required of me.

Therefore, your first response to anything life throws your way is to turn your mind and heart towards God. This can be a brief prayer for help, sitting in quietness to listen, or singing praises of thanksgiving. Quickly run into God's presence. Drink in His water of life by reading His words, the scriptures, be it a verse because that's all you have time for, a chapter, or an entire book. Then meditate on it—think on it—and speak it under your breath until it sinks deeply into who you are as a Christian. Ask Him to open your eyes to see His power and glory in the middle of your daily routines. Remind yourself of

His lovingkindness and give Him praise by singing to Him in your own words—or even those of a song you remember. Humble yourself and bless the Lord. Blessing Him is humbly yielding yourself to Him. Afterall, He is your rock of stability in times of distress, your fortress who shields your heart and soul from negativities, your deliverer who gives you a way to turn distresses into victories, your strength who changes your heart from fears to a strong, trusting confidence in His abilities and love towards you. He shields you, lifts you above your circumstances, and changes your perspective so you can go forward with hope (Psalm 18:2).

Be confident that, when you seek Him, you will find Him, and He will speak to you (1 Chronicles 28:9). It's a truth that bears repeating. If you seek Him, you'll find Him. He wants you to seek Him. He will place Himself right where you can find Him. In fact, scripture says that no man will come to Jesus unless the Father first calls him (John 6:44). Our Father God is the initiator of that desire within us to search for Him. He wants people to find Him.

Trusting your Heavenly Father to give you good things will bring you contentment. When your soul is satisfied with Him, it is easy to be content. My soul becomes satisfied when I give God praise, confidently expecting Him to respond to whatever it is I'm facing. God hears every prayer His children utter, knowing everything we need before we ask, and He loves giving us good things. We simply need to listen and then act on what we've heard.

You can make prayer a part of your life in a variety of ways: in the car, as you go about your daily routines, while playing with your kids, and when laying down in bed before turning out the light at night. God hears every prayer whether it's spoken aloud or thought silently. Remember and record deep within your soul the Lord's promises to lead, guide, and direct you, to save you from every fear, and to deliver you from all harm.

Was my son delivered from all harm when that tree fell? He and his friend quickly jumped out as they saw the tree begin to fall. Then, they walked to the nearest gas station to call me for help, which is why they were not there when the police officer arrived at the scene of the accident. God was faithful to what He had revealed in the vision, and it has become a landmark, a reminder of His grace and loving protection of my son's soul.

You can choose to intentionally pursue God's wisdom with the intent to hear His voice. That means that you are willing to act upon what you've heard. It means you are determined to allow the Holy Spirit of power to help you go around or through the obstacles in your way. When you seek the Lord, He promises that you will find Him. He's not lost; we are before we know Him. Seek His presence in your daily life by being conscious of Him and willing to follow His input. This will lead you into walking in the fear of the Lord—the source of wisdom.

Are you ready to discover what a healthy fear of the Lord is? It starts right here, with time spent getting to know this awesome God who loves you so very dearly. Come with me as I unpack the phrase, "the fear of the Lord," so that you can continue to grow in His wisdom.

# WISDOM BEGINS WITH THE FEAR OF THE LORD

"The fear of the Lord is the beginning of wisdom, and the knowledge of the Holy One is understanding." –Proverbs 9:10 [NEW KING JAMES VERSION]

The Lord was about to redirect our son's steps by intervening in the plans of those in authority over him. This began with six weeks of being told by military officers, "Your son is being discharged and sent home," and the reverse of that, "Your son is being sent back into training." Every day became a test of faith as the Lord taught me to combine prayer with fasting, and rejoicing while acting on His wise counsel.

I certainly had to deal with a fearful mind as my son's situation persisted. It was hard on my emotions, not being allowed to contact our son. During a previous call, he told us that the doctor at the marine base told him he would be discharged and sent home. Yet after he was told that, he was informed that his medical records were lost, and he would be sent back into training.

Anxious thoughts filled my mind when he told us. I found myself praying again. I asked the Lord Jesus, "What do I need to do?" He told me to pay a visit to the recruiter's office to get some updated information. I asked my husband about this strategy without telling him it was God's idea, not mine. He thought it was unnecessary and unhelpful. After some consideration, I decided to be obedient to what the Lord said to me. To act on what I'd heard the Lord say was an expression of the fear of the Lord, an attitude of respect towards Him, and was better than giving into my fears.

The sergeant on duty in the recruiter's office that day immediately called the hospital at Camp Pendleton and put me on the phone with Jeremy. The recruiter was surprised to learn that Jeremy was attending to incoming calls that day. Jeremy was instructed to call me "ma'am, not Mom," just before the phone was handed to me. That call encouraged Jeremy and made me feel elated. It also gave me an opportunity to share with the sergeant what God was doing in my son's heart during his trial of health. A visible shiver went through the sergeant as he said, "I'm so glad I was the one on duty today when you came in to ask for help. I knew when you walked through the door that God had walked in with you." Then the recruiter put me in touch with our son's commanding officer. God's wisdom has a strategy for every situation.

While I continued to build a habit of rejoicing, I often battled fears within my soul. I would have to ask myself a hard question: Did I believe man's word or God's word? The answer to this question would either distress or settle my soul. Man's words would send my heart into a nose-dive of worry. God's Word, on the other hand, would lift my heart up into hope because I trusted my Father God and His infinite wisdom.

Fear—all of us are acquainted with it. Most of us try to avoid it, though we understand it to be a motivator to action. Scripture talks about fear from Genesis to Revelation. Though I haven't counted the verses that say, "do not fear," I've heard ministers say there's a "do not fear" verse for every day of our calendar year. That's three hundred and sixty-five!

Are the uses of the word fear in scripture the same every time? Are they completely different in meaning? Why are we encouraged 'not to fear' while also being encouraged to 'fear the Lord?' Scripture will clarify such a contradiction for us by teaching us how to deal with these two principles of fear.

Grab hold of the trust of God's Word. It encourages us not to enter into fear but to overcome it with the fear of the Lord every day. This may sound like a contradiction. How does fear battle fear? When I did this, I began to understand the fear of the Lord and felt a profound respect for who He was and what He could do, and my newfound understanding of the fear of the Lord changed how I looked at my problems. It became a positive force leading my soul into bold confidence, security, and peace. It also brought me much reassurance both logically and emotionally.

The fear we are so very acquainted with, natural fear, does just the opposite – it leads us to envisioning worse-case scenarios as well as escalating one's anxieties, insecurities and inner emotional turmoil. That's why it's crucial to fear the Lord and not our circumstances.

The first reference in scripture on the topic of fear is in Genesis 9:2. After Noah and his family survived the great flood, God tells them that all living creatures of the earth, the birds of the sky, and even the fish of the sea will be fearful of them. This is true. Animals run away or attack when they are fearful. Fear is a defense mechanism.

The second use of the word fear is found in Genesis 15:1 [NKJV] — "The word of the Lord came to Abram in a vision, saying, 'Fear not, Abram: I am your shield, and the one who will reward you in great abundance.'" The same Hebrew word, *yare*, is used in both the above verses. This view of fear, however, didn't lend itself to defense, but to the Lord's protection and reward toward man.

We see through these verses that fear has been a part of the natural world since the beginning of time. All of mankind must come to terms with this strong emotion. It can be a catalyst that moves us to protective beneficial action when necessary—be it to fight or to flee—or it can be an out-of-control emotion that either freezes us into inaction, or throws us into destructive, harmful behavior.

It's no wonder we are confused when we read in scripture that we are commanded to fear the Lord. We may not be sure of what type of fear to picture. Yet the second verse shows us a different type of fear, the fear of the Lord, that brings a totally different response—one of trusting in who the Lord is and what He promises us. The fear of the Lord is not detrimental to us. Its purpose is to help us live a triumphant life. We must understand the difference between the fear that we have experienced and coped with in the natural world and the fear of the Lord.

The positive side of fear, called the fear of the Lord, is defined in scripture as clean, or pure, and enduring (Psalm 19:9). The purity of this fear produces confidence that the Lord is not just with you but is acting on your behalf to defeat whatever you fear naturally. It turns dangerous situations around for your good, keeps you from harm, and causes life to go well for you. It directly deals with tormenting thoughts of the mind by replacing them with the reality of God's love for us.

The scriptures declare that the fear of the Lord brings many benefits into our lives. Job tells us that we step into God's wisdom when we fear, or have a reverential respect, of Him (Job 28:28). In that type of fear, or respect, we learn to depart from evil. "Evil" simply means anything harmful to us, harmful to others, or disobedient to God.

Understanding what can be harmful—or what is a defiant act against God—and purposely avoiding it is evidence of walking in wisdom and fear of the Lord (Job 28:28). We show the Lord that we fear Him when we have a deeply reverent respect for Him. With that heart stance, we learn more of who God is while gaining a fresh understanding of His character and power (Proverbs 9:10). The fear of the Lord provides us with His fountain of life as a continual resource, and strong confidence in the Lord (Proverbs 14:26). We can be certain of and trust in His protection over us in any situation. We will find ourselves infused with humility as the Lord pours out the essence of His love upon us, granting us riches, honor, and life (Proverbs 22:4). In fact, the fear of the Lord can prolong our lives (Proverbs 10:27). What an awesome benefit!

Walking in the fear of the Lord, then, is to have bold confidence; we are not concerned with what may happen as we abide where He has us. We can know He is with us. We can praise Him and trust His loving-kindness. God cannot lie. He only speaks the truth. Our Father does what He says He will do. We are empowered to endure any difficult circumstance when we trust Him to sustain us, fight for us, and give us success. His plan and purpose for our lives will be fulfilled. We need only to trust Him.

When we develop this positive type of fear, our attitudes and lifestyle begin to reflect these benefits we've looked at. Our lives please the Lord when we demonstrate our confidence in Him. Our trust in Him and our love for Him deepen as we begin to understand that He finds pleasure in pouring out His goodness (Luke 12:32). It affects how we face the difficulties in life. Psalm 22:23 says that those who fear the Lord give Him praise. That's when confident praise becomes the response of our hearts in whatever we're facing. When we demonstrate this confident praise, we also teach our children to fear God and to know our Heavenly Father provides protection. Therefore, we can walk in the comfort He gives because He can remove any residue of natural fear from our hearts. We need to praise Him because praise focuses our hearts and minds on what God can do, not on what men can do. as scripture declares, "if God for us, who can be against us" (Romans 8:31 [NKJV])?

Those of us who fear the Lord respond with gladness when we see God helping others because we also hope in the Lord's Word (Psalm 119:74). It brings health and strength to our bodies (Proverbs 3:7-8). When the Lord pours His Spirit into us, His wisdom, understanding, counsel, and mighty power become available to us. Knowledge of who God is results in a positive, life-sustaining fear of the Lord (Isaiah 11:2). His love for us is wholesome and can completely cast out all tormenting fears (1 John 4:18). God overcomes the natural fear, that fear we know so well in this world, with His love leading us into the fear of the Lord, reverent awe of Him. Fearing God stabilizes our hearts and minds with an expectant hope for all He has promised.

The following powerful scripture passages show us the Lord's response to the fear of God within us. Psalm 33:18-19 describes the Lord God focusing His eye upon those who actively hope in His mercy, and in His ability to deliver from death. Sometimes our soul dies within us from lack of hope, or famine caused by distance from His Word.

Death is not His desire for me or for you! He wants to rescue us from that type of fear that would kill hope.

In fact, He so wants to rescue us that He positions Himself to encamp and surround us with Himself as a protector who hears every prayer, every cry. He desires to give us a heritage of blessings designed to shield us from harm and from fears—just because we chose to fear Him (Psalms 34:7; 61:5; 115:11).

I don't know about you, but that's what I want! So, how do we develop the fear of the Lord in our lives? What steps do we need to take?

Psalm 34:9-22 [NKJV] teaches us how to fear Him— "Fear the Lord, you His saints, for there is no lack to those who fear Him." There is no deficiency, no impoverishment! What an uplifting promise!

Do you ever feel deficient when attempting something new? Building a new skill requires us to listen to instructions and then practice until we develop the needed expertise. Babies learn to walk through repetition. They must try, try, and try again until they get it right. The same is true in developing the fear of the Lord. We learn to know and trust Him. We don't quit after a lackluster attempt. "Want" in Psalm 34:9 [NKJV] stems from a translated word that means "to fail." Failure doesn't mean we quit. It means we need to keep on learning. Learning often requires lots of practice. The next verse tells us that "young lions," or young believers, will experience need, will feel destitute, will grow hungry for solutions, "but they that seek the Lord shall not lack—" they will not fail to receive— "any good thing" (Psalm 34:10 [NKJV]). However, they may presume upon the Lord by failing to do what the scriptures instruct, or by failing to ask for what's needed to overcome their fears. They could also experience lack by asking wrongly or by desiring something that benefits their "passions" (James 4:3 [NKJV]). I've noticed many young believers get sidelined simply because they start off in a rush, run into things that stir up natural fears, get discouraged, and become destitute. The cure for this, of course, is to fear the Lord, to seek His wisdom first which speaks counsel into us, and then to do what He says.

The rest of Psalm 34 gives us steps to take to develop this positive fear of the Lord. We are to become frequent enquirers of God's counsel. Are you asking the Lord for His input into whatever is stirring up fears within you? Ask Him for His wise counsel. Then act on it.

We also need to keep our mouths from speaking guile (Psalm 34:13). That's not a word we use too much in our daily conversations. Guile is speaking in a way that deceives. We too often deceive ourselves when telling our account of a story, leaving out details, or highlighting others to present our own opinion whether it's right or wrong. This sometimes happens in cases of hurt or of a fearful heart. We hear this when someone wants to sway their audience a certain way—newscasters and advertisers use this tactic frequently to sell their story or product. But a believer should not intend to deceive. Deception harms oneself and others.

We need to speak truthfully, "do good, seek peace, and pursue peace" (Psalm 34:14 [NKJV]). This grabs the Lord's attention since His eye is upon His people. His ears are open to our cries. In fact, He swiftly rushes to defend us against our enemies, delivering us by snatching us away, saving us from harm (Psalm 34:15-18). He frees us from restrictive confinement. He establishes us in a safe place. The fear of the Lord delivers us from all afflictions, from all adversity, and from hatred so that our soul can securely trust Him. He releases us from desolation, guilt, and offenses (Psalm 34:19-22). There is a wealth of promises in this passage that affect our reality when we set our hearts to walk, live, and breathe in the fear of the Lord. The fear of the Lord deep within our hearts is a sweet aroma of worship to our Father. Is that what you desire? It's certainly what I want!

Let me once more emphasize the benefits awaiting you as you embrace the fear of the Lord. The fear of the Lord will build your confidence, promote righteous actions, purify your motivations, and empower you to do what you thought you couldn't. He is your source of power, protection, peace, and rest. He brings a refreshing life to your soul. You can feast on His goodness in the presence of your enemies (Psalm 23:5). Adversity doesn't have to bring panic to your soul. Instead, you can walk under His anointed authority. You can learn to embrace His mercy and abundant goodness every day of your life.

Let's walk in the fear of the Lord together, enjoying all these benefits as we choose to give Him our reverence and respect, listening to His counsel and words of help.

# FEAR HAS TWO PERSPECTIVES

"The fear of man brings a snare; but whoever puts his trust in the Lord shall be safe." –Proverbs 29:25 [NEW KING JAMES VERSION]

Years ago, my husband and I lived with our very young children in Germany. One day, when I took our two older sons for an afternoon meetup, I saw the difference between natural fear and the fear of the Lord acting out in my own life. My boys were happily playing on the playground equipment with my friend's children while my friend and I chatted and kept an eye on all of them.

After a while, my friend's daughter along with my oldest, age five, son asked to use the bathrooms. Because the restrooms were close by, we let them go as we watched from the bench. They both came out without either of us seeing them, the young girl returning by herself. After a few more minutes of waiting for my son to return, I asked her where he was. She said he was using the bathroom. I checked the restroom. He wasn't there. I started walking around the large playground, but there was no sight of him.

It seemed like an hour of looking and waiting, when panic began to rise inside of me. I began looking for a police officer or security person to help me in my search. How would I describe my son if I needed to speak German? At the same time, I also began to encourage myself in the Lord. I chose to trust Him to somehow show me where my young son was. More time went by without finding him. We began to walk through the very large park looking everywhere for him.

Praising God for His goodness to me in past times, I looked down the path to see a nicely dressed woman holding the hand of a small boy. It was my son! I ran up to her as she asked, "Are you this boy's mother?" I won't say the harsher things she said to me as she explained that he had walked into the hotel where she worked, approaching her station at the concierge desk to ask for a bathroom. That hotel was at the furthest end of the park and across six or eight lanes of very busy, inner-city traffic.

Still, the Lord knew exactly where my son was at every moment. He kept His merciful, protective hand on him all the way to the hotel and back again. He moved on that woman to walk with my son into the park to see if she could find his mother. My trust in the Lord was repaid with His kindness. My faith in the Lord kept me from yielding to the very natural fear over my son's whereabouts. It enabled me to encourage myself mentally and emotionally in God's merciful ability to reconnect me with my son. I never panicked, though I had great concern. I never feared my son would be forever lost because my God knew exactly where he was.

Natural fear is what we are most familiar with. It is an emotion experienced in anticipation of some specific pain or danger. It is accompanied by a desire to flee, fight, or freeze as we try to become invisible. In some situations, this natural fear can also be a feeling of profound respect for someone or something, helping us to yield to their position of authority or expertise.

Our reaction to fear begins as a strong emotion—such as a painful apprehension—of something about to take place. This sets us up to imagine what will happen. Anxiety may arise as we begin to worry about the things passing through our minds. We may become sleepless or restlessly agitated or even suspicious of people and situations around us. We experience doubt over what action to take as a means to relieve our fear. It can mobilize us, immobilize us, or push us to do what we would not normally do. Sometimes fear is simply a deep reverence or awe-inspiring respect for someone or towards the Lord God, as has been already covered.

In the Bible, King David expressed his natural fear as anxiety of mind and soul due to the threatening voice of his enemy, stirring up in him a desire to flee (Psalm 56:1-8). He tackled the fears of his mind and soul by casting his burden onto the Lord because he trusted God to sustain him (Psalm 56:22). He encouraged himself in the Lord by speaking about what he had experienced. He knew about God's mercy, just as I did while searching for my son.

Fear has two sides—one negative and one positive. To address the negative side of fear, there are at least forty-six times in scripture where the Lord God specifically speaks to us with the words "Fear not, for I am with you," (Genesis 26:24, and Jeremiah 46:28 [NKJV]). We must face our fears before we can either defeat it by rejecting natural fear or overcome it with appropriate action. Laying hold of the fear of the Lord, the positive side, helps us defeat those fears tormenting us.

Natural fear can produce anxiety of mind and soul, physical trembling, and torment of our minds. It can also cause us to react in defense, or it can set us up to fall into a pit of despair as we flee. Sometimes we're caught in an immobilizing snare we need to be rescued from (Isaiah 24:18, Jeremiah 48:44).

Uncontrollable fears over specific things are sometimes known as phobias. Fear can make a person nervous, agitated, fainthearted, or unwilling to assert themselves. The fear we experience in the world brings torment (1 John 4:18). But that doesn't mean we should surrender to it.

When we fail to walk in the fear of the Lord, we can quickly fall into sin. Jeremiah 2:19 informs us that our wrong choices will serve to correct us. Being unfaithful to the ways of the Lord can bring us into a time of instruction, often in the middle of adversity or bitter circumstances due to our unwise choices. The second half of Jeremiah 2:19 says that we should know and realize how utterly harmful it is to us when we reject the Lord our God through disrespect of Him who rules over everything. Giving God due respect leads us into obedience to Him.

Psalm 21:11-13 [NKJV] says, "Teach me Your way, O Lord, and lead me in a smooth path, because of my enemies. Do not deliver me to the will of my adversaries...I would have lost heart, unless I believed that I would see the goodness of the Lord in the land of the living." That is exactly what kept my heart and mind from giving in to panic as I searched for my son. It was also how I coped with my stress years later, during Jeremy's difficulties in the Marines. This became not only a prayer, but a victorious song of triumph the Lord had me sing and dance to around the house whenever fearful doubts afflicted my mind. Every time I danced while singing those words, I pictured the enemy of our souls defeated and under my feet with the Lord Jesus, our victor, dancing with me in joyous deliverance.

One encouraging example of fearing the Lord instead of men is the story of Gideon in Judges six and seven. The passage begins with a dialogue between the Angel of the Lord (that is, Jesus) and Gideon as he threshed wheat under cover of darkness. Gideon feared the Midianites, a formidable foe, would invade Israel. The Lord didn't address him as a fearful man but rather as a mighty man of valor—one who feared the Lord, not man. As Gideon engaged in this conversation, he found himself filled with courage to do what the Angel of the Lord directed. His direction led to a strategic plan of divine wisdom that made no sense to the natural mind. Gideon and another man were to slip into the Midianite camp at night to hear a word of encouragement. That word came through overhearing a Midianite soldier explain a dream that woke him from sleep. In that dream, Gideon, identified as a barley loaf, was coming to defeat them. That word so encouraged Gideon that, at the Lord's direction, he took three hundred men to the top of the hill at night with a clay jar housing a torch in one hand and a sword in the other. Together, they broke the jars. Their torches shone brightly as they lifted their swords and yelled, "the sword of the Lord and of Gideon" (Judges 7:20 [NKJV]). The Midianite soldiers woke abruptly and slayed one another in their panic.

Gideon had courage because he knew God was on his side. Courage is a result of living in the fear of the Lord. We must linger in God's presence to hear Him speak to us of our ability and identity. Just as Gideon engaged in conversation with the Lord, so too must we talk with Him. Our God will correct how we think of ourselves.

God also gives us wise counsel to act on. Gideon took the first steps of obedience while still under the cover of darkness due to the fear of man (Judges 6:25-28). He not only tore down an altar to Baal, a false god, but built an altar to God right where the angel had consumed his sacrifice with fire. We, too, can take steps of obedience to what we hear the Lord speak to our hearts. Gideon also allowed his father to defend him. It was just his earthly father, but he spoke boldly to those who wanted to kill his son Gideon. By asking a wise question, those who were set against Gideon changed their intentions. This reveals how God our Father intervenes on our behalf as well. Questions often change the attitudes of a person's heart, thereby changing their hurtful intentions.

Let your faith in God challenge your natural fear. When the Spirit of the Lord came upon Gideon, he was encouraged to come out of hiding and to gather others to himself. They prepared to rout the Midian army and force them out of their region. God accepted Gideon's further need of reassurance by answering his requests for a sign. These were requests seeking supernatural evidence through natural objects. Gideon's faith strengthened through interaction with the Lord, as does ours.

Success against an enemy of thousands started with the first step of obedience: to lay his sacrifice out upon the rock (Judges 6:19-21). The rock speaks to us of Jesus, the one who gives us a firm foundation. Gideon saw acceptance by God through the fire that came out of the rock to consume it. That fire represents the empowerment of the Holy Spirit. We can have this same assurance, acceptance, and empowerment as we do what pleases the Lord God.

Gideon had gone from hiding in fear to bold obedience. He did what the Lord instructed, thus cooperating with God's strategic plan to remove the enemy's threat. God loves to share His plans with His people. You can experience the same courage that Gideon did when you step past natural fear to do what the Lord says.

Gideon's story, as well as my own, expresses what Psalm 25:14 [NKJV] reminds us: "The secret of the Lord is with those who fear him, and He will show them His covenant." His covenant is an everlasting covenant full of promise. His promise to protect, guide, and increase trust of the Lord to bring comfort to our hearts and courage to our innermost being. We can be confident that the Lord hears our cries for help when we're attacked by threats that would harm or discourage us. He is always ready to act on our behalf. We, therefore, can dwell in His presence daily, gazing at His beauty (Psalm 27:3-4). We can ask Him for counsel. We can laugh in the face of any disaster, both natural and man-made (Psalms 46:2, 52:6). We can trust the Lord will see us safely through.

Every experience of hardship has the potential to strengthen our confidence in the Lord. When we lean into the fear of the Lord, we discover His miraculous ability to help. He gives us strength in times of need. Whenever we lean into natural fear, giving into anxiety and negative emotions, our Heavenly Father understands our weakness. He will still come to help us even when we misunderstand His work-ings. When we recognize His helping hand, we can then declare what He has done for our souls (Psalm 66:16).

Why do we need to ask for the counsel of the Lord when we know He is with us? His answers bring clarity into our lives regarding what to do, when to act, and how to act. His counsel can change our distress into hope in His mercies.

I wish there were another word other than "fear" to define the fear of the Lord. It involves showing Him complete respect and honor and being willing to do whatever He asks of us. I can only some-what compare this fear of the Lord to my respect and honor for my dad. Because of my dad's love for me, he spoke encouragement that helped me overcome my panic when setting out to do something I'd never attempted before. He urged me to confront someone when it would have been so much easier to avoid that conversation. Because he expressed confidence in my ability to do what I didn't want to do, I was successful and learned from the experience. It reminds me of how the fear of the Lord affects my life. God speaks bold confidence into me, enabling me to do what I didn't think I could do. My trust in my dad's love for me helped me overcome my natural fear—just as God's love for me helped me overcome the fear of things only He could control. Those moments became testimonies of His powerful presence intervening in my life.

Some practical steps to take to overcome natural fear begins with acknowledging God's love for you. There is no fear in His love. His love is perfect, completing the confidence we need to cast out all fear (1 John 4:18). Therefore, you can call out to Him. You can tell Him all about your fears. You can throw all your fears at His feet because He cares for you (1 Peter 5:7 NKJV). He knows your fears and how to free you from them. Remind yourself of who He has been to you and what He has done for your soul in the past.

Listen to hear His voice today. What is He saying to you? Write it down so you won't forget. Command your soul to rest in Him (Psalm 116:7-8). As an expression of trust towards Him, speak your praise and thanksgiving to Him. Keep any vows you made before Him. Die to yourself—to doing life without Him to help you.

Jesus said it this way: "Deny yourself. Take up your cross and follow Me" (Matthew 16:24 [NKJV]). Jesus nailed all fear to the cross He died on. Nail any fear you are struggling with to His cross and follow His word. Do the simple step He says to do even if you can't see how it benefits you, it will help you defeat your fear. Just do what He says and then watch what He does in response. Don't forget to give Him praise once you realize how powerfully He has come through for you. Our part is that small—just do what He says, and He will do the rest. His love leads the way to overcoming fear in such powerful ways!

# LEARNING DISCERNMENT

"Those who by reason of use have their senses exercised to discern both good and evil." –Hebrews 5:14 [NEW KING JAMES VERSION]

When I was a kid, my family would fly across the country in my dad's private airplane. I always enjoyed opening the side window to put my arm outside to feel the air. The wind was always stronger outside the airplane window than outside of a car window. The air rippled my skin with its force. I learned about the current of airstreams as we flew along. If I positioned my hand just right, my arm kept its position. If not positioned correctly, my arm would be thrown backwards, downwards, or upwards. I also learned to look at the sky to discern what the clouds meant weatherwise.

Putting my arm outside the window in the rain fascinated me due to the impact the drops made on my arm. Depending on the amount of rain within the cloud, the drops would hit with force or only deposit mist on my skin. Thinking back on this as an adult, I realized how finding the right position for my arm to hold steady amid the airstreams was like finding stability in cooperating with the Holy Spirit of God. Relating the rain to words, we can be hit hard or softly by what others say. We can be so good at discerning (i.e., distinguishing) natural things yet fail in discerning the things of God.

Jesus talked to His disciples about being able to discern the natural signs of the weather (Matthew 9:2-3). God wants us to embrace practical wisdom. Taking note of the weather helps us make wise decisions on what to wear or what outside activities to participate in. Do we need an umbrella? Should we cancel that hike? "Red sky at night, sailors' delight. Red sky in the morning, sailors take warning," is still familiar today. These are simple examples of discernment learned through observation, but how well do we discern the things of God's Spirit?

Discernment is an ability not just to distinguish one thing from another but also the ability to choose wise speech and behavior without causing harm or offense. It is a wise judgment between good and bad.

As a mom trying to discern the Lord's will in what was happening with her son, I often turned to the Lord Jesus for answers and counsel from scripture. The Lord had me fast while praying that His will for Jeremy be spoken into the heart of his commander, and that His word would run swiftly to fully accomplish His will and prosper (Isaiah 55:11). He often directed my attention to verses such as, "No king is saved by the multitude of an army," which encouraged me to understand that no military commander could overrule God's will for my son's life (Psalm 33:16 [NKJV]).

I was learning to discern between my own thoughts and emotions, and the thoughts that came from the Lord as I prayed. His words of direction were so simple to obey. After doing what He would say, I would be amazed at the results.

In the meantime, Jeremy was drawing his own strength and encouragement from the Lord. He was reading the Word of God continuously, praying constantly, and witnessing often. His superiors told him he would be sent home. Then they would tell him he was being ordered back into the Recovery Unit to be sent back into training. These two orders reversed each week—sometimes almost daily. Because he was on his own emotional roller coaster, he asked the Lord to speak to me about his being sent home because he trusted me to hear the Lord Jesus correctly, praying, "Let me hear from Mom first about what Your will for me is." He wanted to hear from the Lord before believing the contradictory words spoken by those over him. He also asked the Lord for an opportunity to call home.

He clung obstinately to the Lord through it all—much to my joy and comfort. Quietly singing to the Lord while on guard duty one evening, a passing officer yelled, "Recruit, what are you doing?" He yelled back his response, "Singing praises to the Lord, sir!" The - officer stammered in surprise then gave the order, "Carry on as you were," before walking on. Such humorous incidents amid emotional upheaval gave him hope that the Lord was at work.

As I turned my heart to the scriptures for counsel, the story of Paul under confinement seemed to leap off the page. Even this great apostle of faith sometimes failed to immediately discern things due to the unpleasantness of his circumstances, just as we often do.

One day in Jerusalem, Paul was speaking of Jesus to a public audience when the crowd reacted in violent disagreement. Roman soldiers rushed in to protect Paul from a potentially deadly beating (Acts 22:22-24). The Sanhedrin Council of priests were called in to question Paul. One of the men of the council gave the order to slap Paul forcefully.

Paul's anger erupted, "How dare you! You whitewashed wall!" (Acts 23:3). His emotions clouded his judgment. The man who had ordered him slapped, the high priest, had full authority to give such a command (Acts 23:1-10). Paul's misjudgment was quickly corrected when he realized his error. He immediately apologized, "I didn't know you were the high priest. Scripture teaches us not speak evil of the ruler of our people." (Acts 23:5 [NKJV]).

Shortly afterward, Paul's discernment clicked in as he viewed the people in the room. He realized there was a mixture of Pharisees, who believed in the resurrection from the dead, alongside Sadducees, who believed there was no resurrection from the dead. This contradiction is what Paul addressed as he began his defense before the Council: "I am a Pharisee, the son of a Pharisee. I'm on trial concerning the hope of the resurrection of the dead" (Acts 23:7 [NKJV]). A riotous disagreement broke out between these two factions.

Once again, to protect Paul, the soldiers swiftly led him away from the shouting council members, thus providing Paul with a peaceful evening, though still under guard. There, the Lord Jesus spoke to him, filled him with courage, and gave him further direction. It wasn't Paul's natural abilities that shifted his circumstances; it was our Father God's protective hand sparing Paul from the people through the wisdom of discernment. Once Paul stopped depending on his limited natural insight, he stepped into a confident peace, operating with wise discernment that directed his words and behavior.

The precious gift of discernment benefits us in a multitude of ways. Wise discernment opens our understanding to know how to proceed with words as well as with action. It rescues us from volatile situations. It helps us live as peaceably as we can with the people around us. When we ask the Lord for help, He sends the Holy Spirit to empower us—especially in times of disagreement as we saw with Paul.

We can more easily experience wisdom's discernment when our emotions are brought under control. We listen for what is true. What do we hear the Holy Spirit whispering to us? What inner promptings from Jesus are we aware of? We can then discern which battle to engage in and how to engage in it. Paul did just that, starting with an apology and ending with an address to all the members of the council. Discernment teaches us to distinguish between our own spirit, the Spirit of God, and any other spirit in this world. The Holy Spirit enables us to discern and perceive as God does.

We need to ask the Lord to help us become sensitive to the counsel of His Holy Spirit. We must keep our focus on the Lord with our ears listening to His words. Both Jesus and the Holy Spirit point us to the Father. We don't want to miss what He has prepared for us. We want to cooperate with Him because His Spirit of truth points us toward the appropriate action to take, not to mention how He ministers to our hearts.

Godly discernment is a gift from God that supersedes natural discernment—just as wisdom from above is far superior to our natural, learned wisdom. Discernment and wisdom must work together in our lives. Godly discernment comes through the knowledge of Him. It enables us to distinguish between what is good and what is best. It helps us make clear-sighted decisions, creating no offense.

Wisdom begins with the fear of the Lord. An outgrowth of wisdom is discernment. Wisdom trains us to discern between what is holy, meaning true, and what is not (Ezekiel 44:23). Discernment teaches us the difference between what is just before God and before man, between what is morally wrong and what is upright in character and behavior. *You* can learn to correctly discern the circumstances or season you are in.

This God-given supernatural ability to judge rightly enables you to distinguish situations from how they may appear to what they are in truth. Discernment helps us identify what the underlying issues are that distress the mind, heart, and soul. Then we can choose to do what is right before the Lord. The skill of discernment must be developed. Scripture encourages every believer to learn to discern through training our senses, or our moral compass, to rightly distinguish between what is good and what is worthless and harmful (Hebrews 5:14). This sharpening of our senses brings awareness to the hidden nature of our circumstances. We can grow in discernment by feeding upon every word proceeding from the Father until we recognize and reject anything that is not from God's Word. We then approach our circumstances with the understanding that comes through discernment. Discernment helps us grow into the image of Christ.

What about you? I encourage you to ask the Lord for wise discernment as you familiarize yourself with scripture to better develop this precious gift.

# SEEING FROM GOD'S PERSPECTIVE

"To know wisdom and instruction, to perceive the words of understanding." –Proverbs 1:2 [NEW KING JAMES TRANSLATION]

We don't know exactly what we will face in our day. I remember one time I accompanied my husband on a business trip to Frankfurt's International Airport. I had no idea what was about to happen. He was there for a simple enough business venture. My husband had to resolve a problem with a grounded airplane as he was the liaison between the airline and Boeing. While he was engaged in his task, I put our toddler in his stroller so we could walk the corridors of the airport. We were heading to a toy store to fill our time by browsing. I vaguely remember seeing a briefcase set beside the trashcan near the door.

Suddenly I heard myself telling my son, "We'll come back to this toy store after we've seen the museum." The Holy Spirit had kicked discernment into high gear without giving me a mental reason, but a clear directive to act on without question.

"Why did I say that?" I wondered as I turned the stroller around to walk in the opposite direction. We had just reached the end of the corridor when an explosion showered debris everywhere. The deafening sound was followed by a shocked silence as smoke rapidly filled the air. People either began to run away from or toward the source of the explosion to lend assistance.

The briefcase I'd seen beside the trashcan had housed a bomb. We did not return to that toy store. When listening to the news in our hotel room later that day, I understood that no one was seriously injured, though some needed medical attention.

"Thank you, Lord Jesus, for such incredible protection to me and our son as well as others!" I prayed with great joy. The Lord—who sees everything—had spoken to me by His Spirit to lead us away from harm.

When we plan our days as I did when walking with my son to the airport toy shop, the Lord directs our steps within those plans (Proverbs 16:9). We can ask Him to tune our ears to heaven so that we hear His voice more accurately and specifically. The Holy Spirit speaks wisdom, understanding, counsel, might, and discernment into us for effective living and ministry to His body. He knows where our plans will take us and is faithful in directing our steps toward what is best for us.

Each of us has the capacity to perceive and experience the goodness of the Lord in our lives. Our plans, thoughts, and decisions for a day often differ from the Lord's. He knows our future as well as our present. He sends His Word into our lives like rain to direct every step, as it says in Isaiah 55:8-11, to accomplish His goodness to us. My son and I certainly experienced God's goodness that day!

The key is to keep our ears attuned to His voice. We do this by keeping alert, waiting expectantly for His prompting and direction. His words act as goads, an instrument to point us in the right direction—much like a shepherd's staff directs sheep back onto the path. Or in my case, what the Lord used with me to redirect my steps away from the toy store to safety. That goad can urge His precious ones forward or rouse us from stillness to necessary action. God's words are full of wisdom used to convict us when we choose wrongly, to lead us into His plans for us, to redirect us away from danger, to comfort us in times of distress and grief, and to encourage us to trust Him.

Let's turn again to scripture to learn how God helps His people see from His perspective. The story of the prophet Elisha and his servant illustrates this in chapter six of 2 Kings. His servant was overwhelmed by the situation they faced. The King of Syria was attempting to invade Israel by surprise. Repeatedly, the Lord God would share with Elisha where the enemy of His people were advancing. Then, Elisha would share God's words with the king of Israel. This eventually became known to the Syrian king who then sent spies out to discover Elisha's whereabouts, intending to take him captive.

Early one morning, Elisha's servant awakened to discover that the city they resided in had been surrounded by the Syrian army. There were horses and chariots everywhere. In a panic, the servant ran with this information to ask Elisha what to do. It is interesting how Elisha spoke to his servant's fearful heart: 'Fear not! There are more on our side than is on their side,' (2 Kings 6:16 [NKJV]). Then, Elisha asked the Lord to open his servant's spiritual eyes to see the armies of God currently surrounding them with His divine protection.

The Lord answered that prayer immediately. Suddenly, the young man saw a vast array of horses and chariots of fire surrounding them on their mountain residence (2 Kings 6:17). That angelic army was acting as a shield of protection around them. They were far more numerous than the army of Syrian soldiers.

Elisha asked the Lord not to destroy, but to strike their enemy with blindness. This turned the threatening situation around completely! Elisha led them in their blind state into a city to feed them with food and water. Afterward, he asked the Lord to restore their vision. Immediately their eyesight was restored. Elisha spoke kindly to them before sending them back to their country to report these happenings to their king.

There are no enemies that can defy God—or His people—though we need His strategy to help us overcome natural fear and open our eyes to see as He sees. The invading army was stronger and greater in number than Elisha and his servant alone. But Elisha knew that his God was more powerful, and his faith became sight when he saw the army God had amassed on their behalf. God, in His goodness, allowed Elisha—and his servant—to see (or discern) the protection of the Lord around them. That's why Elisha could so boldly encourage his servant. He could see clearly. He knew that God protected them, just as He protected me in the airport.

The Holy Spirit empowers those who trust Him to see as He sees and then do as He directs. This doesn't depend on human resources but on heaven's resources. Are you ready to attune your heart to see as God sees, hear His voice, and trust Him enough to obey Him?

Learning to see from God's perspective begins with knowing Jesus, who shows us the Father and gives us His Holy Spirit. We get to know a person when we spend time with him. The same is true in knowing God.

The more I read His words, the better I'm enabled to recognize His voice. The more I pray and sit in His presence, the better trained my soul is to listen to Him and to sense His nearness. The Bible is filled with examples from the lives of God's people who knew God in tangible ways.

Apostle Paul was one of those. We can learn much from Paul's life in scripture. He was no stranger to dealing with the pain and unsettledness of the unknown. On one occasion, Paul encountered something that disturbed him, (Acts 16). As he walked with friends to the place of prayer, a young woman was following them, repeatedly saying, 'These men are the servants of the Most High God, which show us the way of salvation,' (Acts 16:17 [NKJV]). Her words were true, yet Paul was immediately troubled by her repeated declaration. Paul did not immediately respond. This continued for three days, recurring wherever she followed them. I'm sure Paul sought the Lord's input on why her words disturbed his peace of mind and spirit.

Finally, there came the day that Paul turned to her, identifying the spirit of divination speaking through her. In the authority of Jesus's name, he commanded it to leave her. It did. Instantly!

The point I am making with this story is that we must also take our thoughts and feelings to the Lord, just as Paul paid attention to the red flag, he experienced in the form of an internal disturbance inflicted by an outside source. The Holy Spirit enabled Paul to rightly identify the troubling spirit. The Lord gives discernment coupled with His perspective to discern between what is good and what is evil. Paul spoke with God-given authority to free a young woman from a manipulative spirit. There's much more to glean out of this story, but that's another topic.

Just as both Jesus and Paul discerned the spirit of those talking with Him, so we can as well. I remember a time when this type of discernment was made evident to me. As a young adult with an unsatiable hunger for Jesus, I was seeking His presence by prayer and reading the Bible every evening after work. I also would eagerly sit under the teachings of God's Word. One Sunday morning after the congregation was dismissed, the congregants would shake the pastor's hand before exiting the building. When my turn came, I shook his hand as I told him how much I enjoyed his sermon. I asked him if he could remind me of the scripture he had used.

To my surprise, his face immediately turned red as he shouted at me, "How dare you ask for a scripture reference when you haven't attended church all summer!"

Two thoughts went through my mind. First, had he asked, I would have told him I had spent the summer with my grandparents who lived in another state. Second, I realized that the spirit he was speaking from was not his own but influenced by the accuser of God's people. God's perspective laced with love, enabled me to immediately forgive him as I walked out the door. It also set my heart to intercede in prayer for him. It was evident that my request had triggered something in his heart that the Lord was working on.

Seeing through the lens of God's love guarded my heart while rescuing me from any offense of the soul, bad advice, and unfair condemnation due to whatever had been triggered within him.

When we exercise our sense of reason to rightly perceive good from evil, we gain discernment. When natural perception fails us, the Spirit of the Lord is available to open our eyes to see as He sees. He imparts wisdom during times of failure as He did with Paul's inability to see why the woman's words troubled him. The very thing we fail at can become a steppingstone to godly perspective. Though my pastor failed to discern my hunger for the Lord, godly perspective founded upon His love made it easy for me to forgive him.

Decades later, that same pastor tracked me down to have a surprising conversation. His adopted daughter, my best friend through grade school and high school, was dying of cancer. He wanted to make sure I was thanked for bringing her to church weekly, where she gave her life to the Lord Jesus. That had resulted in his family adopting her when the foster care system failed her.

Our difficult conversation so long ago could have put us at an eternal impasse, but God, in His loving kindness, blessed both of us that day. He is good all the time. And as we talked about my friend and his adopted daughter that afternoon. I'm confident we both demonstrated fear of the Lord in our awe of Him. We couldn't see it all those decades ago, but God could see the full picture.

Seeing from God's perspective directs our discernment, overcomes any fear, and brings confident boldness to do as He says. It may be as simple as choosing to give a soft answer to turn away anger rather than voicing grievous words that do the opposite (Proverbs 15:1).

I'm sure you can think of many a time when your words seemed to stir up anger during a conversation. A soft answer indicates a reply that comes with a voice of understanding and from a point of view that rightly perceives what the underlying need is. Sometimes that soft answer is to not respond with words at all.

We need God's perspective to confront things that must be addressed. We should select words that impart value to the person being confronted, thus encouraging receptivity and enhancing the person's ability to hear us rightly. God's perspective is full of wisdom.

With His perspective, life's circumstances become opportunities to see His loving power change threats into rest, discord into forgiveness, and captivity into freedom. It's not achieved by listening to the multitude of voices around you but by listening to the voice of the Lord Jesus. He empowers you with His Holy Spirit during times of pressure, discontentment, complaining, and regret, to see as He sees. At these junctures of life, God's perspective enables us to wisely discern what to do and how to process our thoughts and emotions.

The Lord can direct our actions, words, and skills to help us navigate whatever life throws at us. Having God's perspective helps us trust God. The knowledge gained from His viewpoint will guide us every step of the way.

He loves giving us His wisdom and opening our eyes to see from His perspective. Won't you ask the Lord for this type of wisdom today?

# GROWING IN UNDERSTANDING

"The fear of the Lord is the beginning of wisdom, and the knowledge of the Holy One is understanding." –Proverbs 9:10 [NEW KING JAMES TRANSLATION]

At the age of five, I taught myself to play the piano. I took a hymnal we had at home, turned to a song I knew, and patiently figured out which key went with each note. I understood that the hymnal held songs I had learned in church. With my mom's limited instructions, I learned about the keyboard and which keys went with which notes on the page. After learning to play the songs with my right hand, with my dad's encouragement, I put my left hand on the keyboard to learn where the notes and keys went together for that hand. Essentially, I taught myself how to sight-read the notes and play the piano.

As an adult, I played at weddings and at church off and on for many years. Then at forty, I took piano lessons from a Russian concert pianist who had lost sight in one eye. She told me, "Wanda, you should have had lessons when you were a child. You have such a strong desire to play, but you taught yourself poor techniques that prevent you from playing as skillfully as you desire. Unfortunately, you are no longer that patient child who learned with lots of time on her hands." So true. I have limited skills. Unlearning those techniques was frustrating because my time was filled with raising busy teenagers, preparing Bible studies for ladies' groups, and running a well-ordered home—on top of keeping a good relationship with my husband. My understanding of how to play never fully coordinated with the necessary techniques needed for me to be as skillful as I had desired.

That's how wisdom works as well. Our understanding is limited without the scriptures teaching us how to navigate life. To grow in wisdom is to grow in our understanding. We must understand that God always has the upper hand, the sustaining hand, and the right hand of power and might in any situation we may find ourselves. This understanding that God brings into our hearts decreases the distress of the unknown, gives us release when we trust Him, and grounds us in His Word.

Understanding something implies bringing our intelligence into what we are thinking about. Wise reasoning leads to skillful application of knowledge. We use this understanding in our considerations, learning, and endeavors. A lawyer would never go into a courtroom without first gaining a full understanding of what he needs to do to either defend or refute the case at hand. We do not blindly go into a real estate purchase without first acquainting ourselves with the cost and additional fees involved—as well as the time length required for the purchase. These are natural ways understanding serves us.

The understanding we gain from God's wisdom incorporates our natural insights and intellect with His supreme knowledge. It's interesting that, when God instructed Moses to build the Tabernacle,

He poured wisdom, understanding, and knowledge of all manner into the skilled workman responsible for making the various parts (Exodus 31:3). He gave them detailed insight into *how* to build, complete with designs that enlightened their creative understanding.

He does the same for us today. When we need His wisdom, understanding, and knowledge, He gives it to us liberally. Those who have positions of authority—such as rulers, CEOs, pastors, etc.—should also be people who have wisdom, understanding, discernment, and knowledge to do their jobs well.

Moses's father-in-law, Jethro, is an example of this. When he observed Moses trying to do everything by himself—leading thousands of freed Israelites, judging their issues individually, Jethro pointed out that without help Moses would quickly wear himself out. Then, he laid out a strategic plan. He told Moses to gather well-abled men to help him. He advised Moses to empower them with specific tasks to maintain order and address the people's concerns. Jethro was a wise, business-minded man who understood the need for more manpower. He knew how to instruct Moses to organize the necessary government of the people. I believe he also gave him insightful instruction, advising Moses to choose men to lead groups of varying sizes. He was to seek out leaders of small groups, mid-size groups, and groups of hundreds and thousands.

Moses quickly grabbed hold of his father-in-law's wisdom and understanding by implementing his counsel. He recognized this strategy came from God. Obeying God's commands is wisdom, for they are principles to live by. Understanding comes when God's Word enters our hearts and becomes the foundation we live by (Deuteronomy 4:6). Other people will be able to see His wisdom and understanding in our conduct—in thought, word, and deed. The fear of the Lord is wisdom and refraining from doing what is harmful and injurious (i.e., evil) is understanding (Job 28:28). Trying to lead a nation without help would have been injurious for Moses and the people. Fortunately, he listened to wisdom.

Moses trusted the Lord's wisdom coming through Jethro for organizing nationwide leadership. He also trusted the Lord with the details needed for building the Tabernacle. God's commands are not grievous to those who love him. In fact, God's commands serve us as safety rails.

Much like the bumper guards in a bowling lane that keep the ball from going into the gutter, so too do God's commands spare us from missing what He has prepared for us. Obeying God's commands is wise. We apply wisdom by simply doing what He says. We understand that in the doing, He will direct the impact of our actions to where it needs to be—not in the gutter, but with success. Eventually, those bumper guards can be removed as one grows more skillful. This is true in our growth of wisdom and understanding as well. When we become skilled in understanding how to rightly apply the wisdom God gives us, our capacity for greater responsibilities increases. This doesn't mean we will always get it right one hundred percent of the time. Our Father God winks His eye at our mistakes, picks us up to encourage us, and helps us keep going according to His purposes for us.

Even some of God's most mature people make mistakes. Take Peter, for example. Even though he was a disciple of Jesus, he failed to understood of what Jesus said would take place upon entering Jerusalem at the time of the Passover (Matthew 16:21-23). Jesus would be arrested, tried, and sentenced to death. Peter's response to this was motivated by his personal desire to see his friend and mentor spared this harsh future. Peter verbally rejected this destiny with the words "be it far from you, Lord. This shall not happen to you!" (Matthew 16:22 [NKJV]).

Recognizing Peter's words were influenced by Satan, Jesus looked to Peter and responded, "Get behind me, Satan, you are an offence to Me for you do not value the things that are of God, but those that are of men" (Matthew 16:23 [NKJV]). This was a learning moment for Peter. His words were not his own. His wisdom was worldly. Worldly wisdom, as defined by scripture, involves our emotions and mind-set. Emotions and thoughts of bitter envy, self-seeking, and boasting against the truth promote confusion and harmful things (James 3:14-15). Peter was self-seeking in his words, wanting to spare his own heart from grief. He did not want God's purpose for Jesus to be fulfilled if it meant his friend and teacher needed to suffer a brutal death. He boasted against the truth by saying 'this shall not happen to you' (Matthew 16:22). No doubt, his heart was thrown into confusion at the same time he spoke those words.

Yet after Jesus rose from the dead, one of His first interactions with His disciples was to gently encourage Peter to not give in to bitterness of the soul and to not think unjustly about himself. He lovingly encouraged Peter to be a leader, to tend to other souls by teaching the words of life to them—words about Jesus. His words brought peace to Peter's self-condemning heart. Peter's testimony continues to bring an understanding of God's mercy to those who hear it.

Peter may not have understood the wisdom of God at the time Jesus was cluing in the disciples about what was to take place, but it did indeed come afterwards. Sometimes we must wait until understanding comes through the things we experience. Understanding will provide us with an ability to do something successfully. Peter successfully overcame his shame of misunderstanding and more.

Success comes as we learn through trial and error, such as learning to play the piano. I gained some skill when I taught myself, yet I gained so much more under the instruction of that concert pianist. All skills take time and repetition to develop.

It takes coordination and oftentimes insight to see ahead. An architect may see the overall design and plan while an engineer sees the details regarding how it all needs to come together. Both have wisdom and understanding in their specific skillset. Understanding God's ways means that we see beyond our circumstances to grasp His purposes *in* our circumstances. Wisdom will give you a comprehension of what needs to be done and the knowledge to do it. The Lord will show you what resources may be needed. Then use your God-given intelligence to apply the knowledge of what you now understand. Ask Him for understanding—just like you've learned to ask Him for wisdom.

Perhaps you can stop right here to take a moment to think about whatever it is you need understanding for. Write out what God speaks to you. Is there some direction that gives you an understanding of how to go about it? If so, trust the Lord as you step out into the obedience of His wisdom and understanding.

# KNOWING GOD

"Through your precepts I get understanding; therefore, I hate every false way." – Psalm 119:104 [NEW KING JAMES VERSION]

I've grown to know the Lord over the course of my life. One memory of many comes to mind from when I was first getting more acquainted intentionally with the Lord. I was twenty-something at the time. It's a memory that taught me how very personal He is. It also taught me that He has control in unexpected situations.

I spent the day visiting my sister in a neighboring city. Heading home late that evening, I talked to the Lord as I drove, bemoaning the fact that I had not given myself time that day for prayer and praise. Halfway home, in the middle of nowhere, the gas pedal of the car dropped useless to the floorboard. I tried lifting it with my foot. No success. Unable to use that pedal, the car gradually lost speed. I headed the car to the side of the road, drifting to a stop. I let out an exasperated, "Lord Jesus, I'll be stuck until morning!"

In that moment the Lord distinctly whispered, "I thought you wanted to spend time with me." In shock, I laughed as I lifted my voice in response by singing to the Lord. His Presence instantly became strong around me.

I'm not sure how much time went by before I heard someone tapping on the window. I opened my eyes to see a young man with a smile. I rolled down the window a bit to hear him say, "I'm Brad. I'm here to I help you." This was very welcome, and I explained what the issue was. He asked me to pop up the car's hood, which I did. When he came back to the window, he asked if I had a flashlight. I didn't.

"That's okay," he said. "Do you have a hairpin?" That I had, and I handed it to him. Hairpin in hand, he went back to the front of the car, leaned over the top of the engine, and went to work. Before long, he finished, and Brad came back to the window.

"When you get home," Brad said, "tell your dad I put the hairpin into the hole of the gas pedal linkage where the cotter key had fallen out. Do you want me to follow you home for safety?"

I told him I would be fine. Again, he stated what he had done as a temporary repair and emphasized that I should tell my dad as soon as I got home. I wondered how he knew I was going home to my parents' house rather than to the apartment I had moved out of. But it was no matter. I waited for him to drive off before aiming my car back to the road for the rest of the drive home. While I waited, the lights of his Volks Wagen Bug flashed brighter than normal then went dark.

I turned around quickly to look more intently at my surroundings. That's when I realized that Brad and his car had not driven away at all. They had disappeared!

The Lord had sifted through my "complaint" to see the real issue—my desire to spend time with Him. Then He proceeded to arrange my circumstances for that to happen. All I had to do was lean into that moment with Him. My part was to respond with worshipful obedience. His part was to provide the solution needed for the situation He had created for me to get to know Him better.

In every circumstance, there is an opportunity to become more knowledgeable of the Lord and to better understand His ways.

When I arrived at my parents' home later that evening, they told me that a glow had come in the door before I entered. That was odd enough. Then, Dad, who was a mechanic, told me it was impossible to reach the gas pedal linkage by bending over the top of the engine. It was not possible either to see that tiny hole without a flashlight on a dark night—even if he'd been laying underneath the car as he should have been. The next day he found that hairpin right where Brad had placed it. The Lord had sent an angel in human form on a mission to repair my car just because I desired to spend time with Him!

To know the Lord causes us to live by His precepts—by His commands. His precepts teach us how to live safely and how to rightly approach Him with confident faith. We come to Him when our hearts are open to receive and return His love. Scripture instructs us to live peaceably with others. His precepts teach us how to do that with graceful attitudes and loving forgiveness. We treat others as we want to be treated, with love and mercy. Mercy brings balance to justice. We learn His ways slowly, "precept upon precept, line upon line, here a little and there a little," through practicing His way of living until it becomes a natural part of who we are (Isaiah 28:10-13 [NKJV]). We learn not to fall backwards, not to be broken, snared, or taken in by what is harmful and untrue.

A part of the learning process is meditating on who God is, what He speaks to us through the scriptures, and how to realistically apply His words to our lives. It stands to reason, then, that those who don't understand the intent behind the scriptures take some passages out of context. For instance, Jesus told his disciples that it would be better to cut off the right hand and cast it far away if it brings them to an offensive action, rather than they end up in hell. Of course, He didn't mean that literally. It would show a misunderstanding of the principle He was teaching to do so. Jesus used those words to illustrate our responsibility to take control of our thoughts and emotions leading us to offensive behaviors. Cut off and cast those thoughts far away before you act on them. He did not teach mutilation of the body as a preventative.

Counselors deal with these self-harming behaviors routinely. Such behaviors do not originate with God. Aligning yourself with God's principles of life, through the grace of the Lord Jesus Christ, brings us into His healing, security, and overcoming power. The Bible is our manual for living.

Many items come with instruction manuals or booklets. Some of us read those manuals, but more do not, preferring to figure out how to operate or put together the device or furniture by trial and error. I remember when, years ago, my husband and sons were trying to fix a problem with our desktop computer. Gradually, they became more and more frustrated about how to apply the solution.

Quietly, I picked up the desktop manual to read through it. As I flipped a page to continue reading, I thought I understood the problem and how to resolve it from what I read. I asked my husband if he had tried what the manual said. He rolled his eyes because he knew I understood very little about computers, but he gave it a try anyway. Immediately the computer started functioning as it should. Reading the manual resolved the issue.

This is true of the scriptures as well. As we read, meditate, pray, and seek counsel from God, we find solutions for many aspects of our lives. That's one reason why God has given us Bible teachers, preachers, missionaries, and theologians. We need these men and women of God to explain His word to us so we can understand His instructions of how to live and receive His blessings. We need to know the "why" of the purpose behind the "how" in the instruction.

There is wisdom in many counselors, and yet, the ultimate counselor is God. He has given us the Holy Spirit, who leads us to Jesus, who shows us the Father. The more we read the Bible for ourselves, the more the Holy Spirit can teach us His truths and principles.

When God's Word penetrates our hearts, it brings understanding of who He is. His truth illuminates the actions we need to take or the words that we need to speak. God's understanding is without end. We can never bring to Him a situation or problem that's beyond His ability. He knows the details of any given situation that we do not. It is a wise man who not only hears but increases in learning by acting on the wise counsel and instruction found in the word of truth (Proverbs 1:50).

Step one is to pay close attention to the teachings of scripture. They give us an understanding as to the "why" or the principle of living. Step two is to apply our hearts to understand the "how," or the action to make it work in our lives.

When we understand the wisdom of obeying God's principles, that knowledge brings a pleasing peace to our souls. We find preservation in the rich resources of scripture. They become a guard to our lives, shielding us from things that harm as well as from the things that lead to perversions of the truth (Proverbs 1:10-12).

When we become familiar with the words of truth, we may find that we are learning to hear and recognize the voice of God. Knowing what He has written down for our instruction and encouragement helps us know when He is speaking to us. He never violates His written words. He never says things contrary to His instructions found in the pages of the Bible. You will learn to hear and distinguish His voice from your own when you act on what He has told you.

Sometimes He will speak firmly enough that we don't even question what we've heard because we know it is Him. This was true when I discerned the need to remove myself and my son from that toy shop in Frankfurt's airport. It was so firmly spoken that my spirit within me immediately responded with a willingness to do what I'd heard.

Becoming familiar with the way God speaks to your heart will help you distinguish between His voice and yours. He knows we learn sometimes through trial and error, so remember that He redeems our mistakes just as He redeems our lives. In other words, He can use our mistakes to train our hearing.

Thomas Edison is recorded as having said of his mistakes while working with electricity, that every mistake is a lesson learned in what *not* to do again. We can have that same attitude. Instead of giving up and relying on others to hear for us, we must learn what wasn't His voice, what wasn't in agreement with the scriptures, and make a note not to do that again!

Understanding comes as we experience God's presence in our daily lives. Sometimes it comes quickly; other times it grows slowly. The longer we live, the wiser we should become. Also, our understanding becomes greater (Job 12:12). The limitations of human reasoning and understanding is far surpassed by God's infinite wisdom and understanding. The counsel of His wisdom, knowledge, and understanding brings the strength to live purposefully into our lives.

In learning to recognize His voice, we should try to respond in obedience. Do or say what He speaks to us. This builds a confident trust in God. Trust establishes a desire to please Him as we navigate every area of life with wise understanding. The surrender of our natural wisdom to His divine wisdom enhances our capacity to hear Him accurately.

Consider these truths found in scripture: the Lord God shares His hidden counsels with us as we walk in the fear of the Lord; as we walk in that reverence of respect (Psalm 25:14). We develop discernment between our own will and His for us through the teachings we find in His Word (John 7:27). We distinguish the purity of God's love from our limited expressions of love (John 14:21). His love empowers us to ask boldly for wisdom from above, because we know and trust Him.

God reveals Himself to us through the scriptures. We gain understanding when we meditate on His Word. To meditate simply means to think about it, to speak it to yourself quietly, asking for a better understanding of what it means. It can be as simple as the verse that says, "you shall not steal" (Mark 10:19 [NKJV]) or more complex, such as: "you shall love others as you love yourself" (Matthew 22:39 [NKJV]).

Ask the Lord what you need to do to love yourself like He loves you. He may show you ways to forgive yourself for mistakes, for words spoken that you regret. Speak His forgiveness over your soul. It will free you from the anguish of those memories. Knowing God and living in the understanding of His principles changes your behavior and thoughts into those that please Him. You will be amazed at how His truth leads you to safety and stability.

# AN ESTABLISHED HEART

"My heart is fixed, O God, my heart is fixed: I will sing and give praise." –Psalm 57:7 [NEW KING JAMES VERSION]

Again, an unsettling report came from the commanding officer presiding over Jeremy's case. Major Morgan called one day to inform me of his final decision. He had decided that Jeremy was to be sent back into training.

"Why?" I asked in shock.

"Because" he explained, "Jeremy suffered from heat exhaustion, not heat stroke." This was apparently a much less significant ailment, and the major deemed him ready to serve.

I admit I immediately got upset with the major. I informed him of all the symptoms my son had explained having, and how they differed from that of heat exhaustion. The major insisted that Jeremy would be fine in the training. However, he gave me his personal phone number in case I had any further concerns, which I certainly did. I hung up the phone with an aching, questioning heart. Had I misheard what the Lord had been saying to me? Had Jeremy misheard what the Lord had said to him about two delays?

I leapt into prayer once again. Not long into crying out to the Lord, I heard that still soft voice of my Savior firmly say, "Call the major back. Apologize to him for venting. Then ask him to investigate what's happened to Jeremy's missing medical records." This was God's counsel and wisdom. Jeremy had mentioned that his medical records had gone missing. Humble obedience was required.

"Was that me?" I wondered. "Or was it really the voice of the Lord?" I could only know for certain by acting on it.

Back on the phone, the major was cordial. I apologized for my words and attitude. Next, I asked that Jeremy's medical records be investigated since I'd been informed that they were missing. His interest was immediate. He assured me he would start an investigation within the next week. The Lord's strategy of wisdom was a simple question that soon made an impact on the whole situation.

The wisdom that comes from God establishes our hearts. The things we desire, the values we hold on to, the lifestyle of listening to Him, and the obedience to follow through become ingrained in our character. A heart fixed on the Lord is established in security regardless of the circumstances. Turning to scripture establishes trust in Jesus, who is called the Word (John 1:1). He is our firm foundation.

Disturbances present themselves in many forms, making it hard to hear God's voice or to understand the counsel of scripture. An intrusion can be healthy or unhealthy. Healthy intrusions must be understood if we are to give our time, attention, and ability to them. Perhaps the intrusions are coming from stress, and relief is needed. Perhaps a boundary needs to be set, or perhaps there is a need to rest and concentrate on the task to be accomplished.

However, a disturbance is unhealthy when we fixate on its need, problem, or busyness. The wrong focus can allow it to consume our thoughts, energy, emotions, and time—all without beneficial results. Anything that creates mental confusion, unsettledness in mind and emotion, or anxiety can quickly become unhealthy for a person's soul.

We are all familiar with the stress of a long "To Do" list with too little time in our day to complete it. We may struggle with an attitude of stubbornness, or a feeling of being pressured by others to say, do, or act in a certain way that is uncomfortable or that we disagree with. When you feel uncertain, confused, impatient, or perhaps are feeling too comfortable with where you are in the moment, your heart needs to be established in hearing the Lord through scripture and prayer. He promises to give you the understanding of what you need.

We have a choice in these moments to remain firmly settled on the foundation of Christ Jesus by seeking first His counsel—or to yield ourselves to the disturbance. We find an example of this in the story of Mary and her sister, Martha (Luke 10:39-42). Martha had invited Jesus to come into her home where He found her busy preparing food to serve her guests. Mary, however, chose to sit at Jesus's feet to converse with Him. When Martha complained about what she presumed was Mary's laziness, Jesus corrected her viewpoint. Mary had chosen the better thing—to listen to Him. He was Mary's focus. Mary had chosen to see the importance of having Jesus, the Son of God from heaven, available to talk with. She set her attention wholly on hearing what He had to say. She refused to let the pressures of busyness delete her focus of heart from Jesus. This is not to say that it was wrong for Martha to focus on meal preparation. Yet to criticize another for not joining her in the tasks she'd assigned herself was unjust. Jesus identified the condition of Martha's heart as distracted by troubled thoughts of busyness.

Established hearts are determined to maintain their relationship with God without fluctuating. Had Martha chosen to sit at Jesus's feet to enjoy His presence, no doubt He would have made room for and helped her get her tasks done without feeling so pressured.

On days when I have too much to do, if I surrender my "To Do" list to the Lord Jesus first thing in the morning, His guidance determines which thing I should start with first. With that one task done, I ask Him what the second task should be. Instead of having no time in my day to accomplish all of it, His counsel helps me get the entire "To Do" list accomplished with time to spare.

This particular result has repeated itself so many times that I've learned to trust Him to order my especially busy days. He rearranges my "To Do" list while including time for rest. His order is more beneficial than when I set my own order. When we ask, He responds to us with a merciful answer steeped in wisdom (Psalm 27:8).

When anxiety, pressure, or stress hits you, give yourself time to have a conversation with the Lord. Prayer is a two-way conversation with Jesus. He will calm your heart. An established heart prevents unhealthy distractions that try to hijack your emotions and energy. Sit at Jesus's feet and let prayer calm and comfort your heart.

As an exercise, try writing out all that is distracting you (that "To Do" list). Now present it to the Lord. Ask what on that list you should start with and do what He tells you to do even if it is the lowest thing on that list. Don't be like Martha who afflicted her mind with self-made distresses. leading her to vent her complaints about her sister to Jesus. His rebuke corrected her attitude. His rebuke corrects ours. She engaged in unhealthy thoughts. Those thoughts made her feel overly responsible, disturbed her peace of mind, and disquieted her soul. Uncontrolled thoughts stole her internal peace. Her improper perspective undermined the opportunity she had to spend quality time with Jesus.

Just like Martha, I sometimes find myself struggling with the responsibilities I've placed upon myself. When that happens, I ask the Lord to help me understand things from His perspective. His way of engaging with life reveals His wondrous works while guarding my heart from self-inflicted distress (Psalm 119:27).

One way to guard the stability of your heart is to worship Him. Worship helps establish your heart in the Lord. Singing songs of praise or simply telling Him how thankful you are for His answers to prayer, peace of mind, love poured out, etc. shifts your focus away from turmoil into His secure peace. Reading scripture brings comfort as well as counsel. In fact, you can turn what you're reading into songs of worship. Singing scripture and hymns can relieve your soul by bringing your mind back to God's faithfulness. Singing praise will help you step into His strength with joy. A sacrifice of praise can be a leap into confident faith in Jesus. Your soul will be encouraged by the words you hear yourself singing to Him.

Music affects our emotions in a positive way. It has been known to spark creativity, relieve pain by relaxing one's breathing, releasing endorphins (that "feel-good" chemical), and focusing our attention. It increases physical activity, or slows it, depending on the tempo. It even helps with memory. Of course, all these things are true because God has created all good things. When we worship, we also remember just how much God our Father loves and cherishes us. Best of all, we are reminded of who He is to us—our strength and redeemer. Isn't God good for creating the beauty of worship?

Establishing our hearts upon the Lord, both through worship and spending time in His word, fills us up with His Holy Spirit. When you do these things, you will find yourself singing melodies of truth that carry through your day. You will find your faith building towards the Lord Jesus, and thoughts of thankfulness coming to mind (Ephesians 5:18b-20).

Life is full of distractions with a plethora of influences, but we have a choice. It's not easy to keep a corner of our hearts alert to sense God's presence, but it is doable. When we consistently bring ourselves to Him, it becomes easier to be aware of Him. The demands of life can distract us from our relationship with God. However, rightly handled, those demands can be the best ladder to God's presence. Praise-filled singing will help keep your heart filled with the Holy Spirit throughout the day and all its demands. Are you ready to start worshipping the Lord? Let Him hear your voice daily and watch as your distress bows to His wisdom.

# THE BENEFITS OF WISDOM

"For wisdom is better than rubies, and all the things one may desire cannot be compared with her." –Proverbs 8:11 [NEW KING JAMES VERSION]

Instead of waiting a week, the major started to investigate that very afternoon. He called the hospital's Recovery Unit to speak with our son. Jeremy, at that exact moment, was feeling very discouraged, asking the Lord for some sign of encouragement and confirmation that he would indeed be sent home. An officer ordered him to "man the phones." Would you believe that the very first call he took was from the major asking to speak with him? This was a fast answer to Jeremy's prayer for encouragement. The major reversed his earlier order of the day by commanding that Jeremy stay put in the Separation Unit until the investigation was complete.

When the major called me back to inform me of his executive decision, a wave of relief flooded me! Not only had the major heard my request but he had acted on it more promptly than expected. Also, he asked appropriate questions that confirmed Jeremy's medical report was indeed lost by those attending it. Such a display of God's wisdom flowing into this whole situation through the major filled me with gratitude.

The major explained to me how he had had a recruit the year before in a similar situation. He had ordered that young man back into training. That recruit's life ended before his training was completed. The major did not want Jeremy to have the same fate. Therefore, he was determined to find Jeremy's medical report. If unsuccessful, then he would advise the doctors to discharge Jeremy due to health concerns. He told me that if the doctors would not agree, he would go over the head of the Medical Unit to the four-star general to preserve Jeremy's life. I was grateful for the major's wise actions. It was clear to me that God had set up the right major to carry out His will. All I had to do was obey God's wise counsel by apologizing on the phone. Our part is simply obeying. God's part is to do what we cannot do, and He is sovereign.

Obedience to the Lord causes us to grow in wisdom, which helps us know God more fully. Knowing Him increases our understanding of His ways. A person who knows God gains insight to the purpose he has been created for. Living out of that purpose deposits a sense of fulfillment in our hearts and pleasure in God's. In learning to understand His ways and what pleases Him, we develop a passion for the scriptures, teaching us to recognize His voice. Discernment develops, enabling us to distinguish between what is right and wrong morally and spiritually. Seeing from His perspective reveals what will benefit our lives and what will harm us.

When wisdom enters our hearts and the knowledge of God has become pleasant to our souls, then discretion begins to preserve us. Understanding His ways guards our conduct as well as our words (Proverbs 2:10-11). We begin to imitate Jesus—acting like Him. His loving kindness deposited within us guides our hearts towards merciful forgiveness when others offend us with words or deed.

Wisdom protects and rescues us from harm. It expands our knowledge of God and His purpose. Wisdom leads us away from perversities and falsehoods. It will quiet our complaints and soothe unpleasantness (Proverbs 2:12-13). Our conduct and conversations transform into wholesome things, things that promote peace and honor in the hearts of others and ourselves. Wisdom brings godly strategy in the face of adversity, affliction, calamity, distress, wrong choices, and evil practices. It affects our reactions to such unsettling situations that arise when we ask to see from God's perspective rather than our limited, natural viewpoint.

One day, when living in Kuwait, I pushed my grocery cart through the store with my son in its seat when a policeman took hold of the cart to push it for me. He refused my insistence that I didn't need his service. This continued all the way through the store, at the check-out register, and to my car where he helped me put my groceries into the trunk. I thanked him, expecting him to depart. At that point, he directed me to get into his police car. Perhaps I was foolish to do so, but I respected the authority of the badge he wore and obediently got into the car. When asking him why and where we were headed, he told me to be patient.

When he pulled the car into a vacant lot, I felt the Spirit of the Lord rise within me, and I turned boldly to him. With great authority, I demanded he turn the car around to drive us back to my car. He immediately agreed though he took a photograph of my son and I first.

This is an instance that I look back on as a lesson in discernment, distinguishing between what was right and what was potentially problematic. I cannot say even today what his intention was. I only remember how strongly the Holy Spirit spoke through me to him prompting his immediate turnaround. God's ability to keep us safe as we practice wise discernment through our experiences can always be trusted.

I failed, due to my natural respect for a position of authority, to discern that there was no real reason for me to get into that police car. Yet wisdom prompted discretion, giving me courage and authority to speak in such a way that the situation was immediately corrected. One of the benefits of wisdom this story illustrates is that wisdom leads us to safety, just as it led me and my son back to the safety of our car. Wisdom provided me with God's strength and a blessing of courage, the force I needed to move forward into safety (Proverbs 8:14).

Another benefit of wisdom is its ability to bring longevity and honor to our lives. It adds length to our days along with riches and honor, pleasantness, and peace (Proverbs 3:16-17). How can it do that? It affects the choices we make. We can wisely choose to avoid immoralities, excesses, harmful influences, and hardships, for example. Wise choices result in peaceful stability of heart and soul. When God's supernatural peace replaces our anxiety, we can live confidently before the Lord (2 Peter 1:5-11). God our Father will promote and honor us whenever we act wisely. Wisdom increases our influence with others as God's grace and favor rest upon us (Proverbs 4:7-10). Furthermore, wisdom makes us mindful of our words and attitudes, much like when I was urged to speak boldly in that police car.

Wise conversations are filled with truthful kindness rather than indulgent, crude, or condescending words. Wisdom can replace an attitude of pride and arrogance with that of humility and grace. God resists the proud while giving grace to the humble (Proverbs 8:13, James 4:6). Therefore, we should choose wise words to promote wholeness, healing, and reconciliation. Wisdom also asks that we honor those we find difficult because it's how the Lord God treats us. He doesn't routinely point out our faults but speaks to us as dear children whom He loves. His example of wise speech can become our way of speaking. To practice speaking wisely, we should be truthful, avoiding words that inflict harm. Refuse words that twist the truth into a lie or those that distort what is good (Proverbs 8:7-8).

Wisdom from above increases our capabilities by revealing what God wants us to know in whatever situation we are facing (Proverbs 8:12). He knows what is needed. His knowledge includes details that we are unaware of. We find His counsel when we ask for His wisdom. God makes His wisdom known to us so that we can have a proper understanding. It comes with the strength to apply it rightly (Proverbs 8:14).

Just like God poured wise understanding into the skillful wood-workers, knowledge into the gold and silversmiths' expertise, as well as into the seamstresses in the days of Moses, He does the same for us today when we ask for His wisdom. The Lord brought those workers together to build the tabernacle, each doing his or her part. The same is true in our lives. Today, He can bring wisely skilled people into our lives who will help us accomplish what needs attending to.

Wisdom will aid us in the positions of authority we hold, be it as parents, teachers, businessmen, leaders in a church, or those in a government position (Proverbs 8:15-16). God can give us the wisdom required to overcome difficulties, relate well to the ones we lead, and to exercise our authority wisely and humbly. God's law of kindness should be seen in our relationships. With wisdom, we have the ability to maintain what's been overcome and accomplished. It gives us sound judgment to govern our lives in the light of God's Word.

Through wisdom, our hearts embrace the disciplines of truth. Wisdom's discipline will cause you to become aware of the daily promptings of the Holy Spirit (Proverbs 8:34-35). Do you desire for your heart to be protected and hedged with the Lord's safety net, His truth? Then seek His wisdom as your shield. Build your life on the pillars of His Word (Proverbs 9:1, 24:3). The Lord's wisdom will influence your thoughts, attitudes, behavior, and decisions. In turn, it will cause you to be a positive influence in the lives of others. You may find yourself speaking wise counsel into their times of confusion, bringing them to the Word of the Lord to restore their joy.

Take note of the times you've heard wisdom from the Lord and write down the outcome! When those testimonies replay in your thoughts and conversations, you will grow in His wisdom. That's a part of the reward of wisdom. It will grow your character as your testimonies of His wisdom expand. Ask the Lord today to show you how wisdom has already benefited your life. Now thank Him for what He has done.

# WISDOM'S EXCELLENCE

"I have heard of you, that the Spirit of God is in you, and that light and understanding and excellent wisdom are found in you." –Daniel 5:14 [NEW KING JAMES VERSION]

As the major launched an investigation to find Jeremy's medical records, we all had to endure a long week of waiting. I had prayed over this situation all that I could. Every time I started to pray again the Holy Spirit would remind me to rejoice! My prayers had already been heard. Now was not a time to intercede still more, but a time to stand in expectant faith.

God's wisdom is always excellent. Whenever my heart felt unsettled, the Lord would suggest that I go for a walk. All creation speaks of God's powerful ability. The trees lift their hands in praise to the Lord. The clouds reminded me how large a hand God must have to hold this world in His palm. And they reminded me of the vision of His mighty hand scooping Jeremy out of the Marines to be a man of peace rather than war. Why fear what man can do when God is so much bigger—immensely bigger—controlling all we can see and even beyond.

We see the excellence of wisdom in our lives when it opens our understanding to God's perspective. Wisdom becomes plentiful when we simply ask God for it, just as I had been doing throughout this stressful time. He reveals to us His intelligence, desires, character, and presence.

In the book of Matthew, Jesus famously said, "Come to me, all you who labor and are heavy laden, and I will give you rest. Take My yoke upon you and learn from Me, for I am gentle and lowly in heart, and you will find rest for your souls. For My yoke is easy and My burden is light" (Matthew 11:28-30). He calls us to walk in the wisdom from above. His invitation gives a description of God's wisdom, how to acquire it, and how to utilize it.

When we are saved, the Spirit of God reveals the gospel, and we receive the salvation of our Lord Jesus Christ. He shows us the Father, and the Spirit teaches us to live in a way that pleases Him. The triune God works seamlessly and brings restful satisfaction to our souls. He also allows wisdom to flow into our lives as we look expectantly to Him for the wisdom we need.

God desires us to live daily approaching Him. When you think of true wisdom, do you consider its excellence? Or do you think of it as a characteristic, skill, intelligence, or mainly a characteristic of the God who created you? God, in His wisdom, calls out to us in the gates, or places of business, and as we come or go in our daily routines (Proverbs 8 :2-5).

The wisdom of God is available to all ages, both men and women, and to the simple as well as the foolish. Wisdom speaks the truth into our hearts. As we ask the Lord for wisdom, it is given to us so we may excel in living life to the fullest. Excellent wisdom will flow into our lives, made possible by a deep relationship with our Heavenly Father and through Jesus, the source of that wisdom (1 Corinthians 1:30). When wisdom flows through our lives, it is accompanied by an understanding of what to do and how to respond or proceed.

The excellence of wisdom is a valuable quality that scripture compares to the value of gold and rubies (Proverbs 8:10-11). No earthly thing of value can compare to the value of divine wisdom. This valuable quality of wisdom pours into us through the fountain of Jesus's life housed within a believer. The secret of growing in the excellence of wisdom is to drink daily from that fountain by spending time with Jesus in prayer and in scripture. Scripture will teach us to live uprightly. Wisdom gives us the understanding to do it with excellence, bringing honor to the Lord. He blesses us by adding more wisdom to what He's already given.

Thus, like Daniel in the verse at the start of this chapter, others will notice and acknowledge the wisdom and understanding you walk in. The qualitative value of wisdom provides you with understanding, counsel, might, knowledge, and fear of the Lord (Isaiah 11:2-5). These excellent attributes of wisdom will help you avoid wrong judgment because you will see a situation from the Lord's perspective. Wisdom will help you discern what you hear and to rid yourself of what is untrue. Truth, in turn, will help your heart rest in the peace that comes through wisdom—even when facing difficult circumstances or relationships. Wisdom judges with righteousness and faithfulness to the Lord. All the treasures of wisdom and knowledge are hidden in Jesus (Colossians 2:3).

When I think of the excellency of God's wisdom, I understand that His wisdom was put on display in creating the heavens and earth. His strategy wasn't haphazard, but orderly. Each new creation progressively supported the next one. We have in Christ Jesus this wise knowledge and an understanding of how to live and build, step by progressive step. We have received the righteousness of Christ Jesus by believing in Him. His righteousness enables us to live by the moral principles of our Father in heaven. We become more and more like Jesus as we set our heart's focus on Him, choosing to listen to His wisdom. We then live in that wisdom, as Jesus did by speaking every word and doing every deed He heard and saw His Father speak and do. Jesus is the embodiment of wisdom's excellence. Our good God gladly and freely gives wisdom to us when we ask Him for it.

We also see the excellence of wisdom at work in the life of Daniel when King Nebuchadnezzar had a dream that the wise men of his realm could not interpret (Daniel 4). Daniel was called into the king's presence and asked if he could give the interpretation. He not only could but he also began with merciful words expressing his heart-felt desire that the dream's judgment would be directed at the king's enemies rather than towards Nebuchadnezzar. Then he said exactly what the Lord revealed to him about the dream. Daniel followed the interpretation with a word of counsel that King Nebuchadnezzar paid attention to. He followed that counsel for a year before yielding once again to the pride in his heart, which resulted in mental illness. His pride led to the dream becoming a reality in his life. Wisdom then, as seen in this story, not only gave Daniel an ability the others did not have but provided the king with a strategy to side-step mental illness for as long as he would follow wise counsel.

From my own life, I recall when I was Vice President of the American Women's Club in Frankfurt, Germany. I organized a gala to raise funds for training a dog to help a child struggling with Multiple Sclerosis. I felt out of my element. The team I had were volunteers with the goal of fundraising by contacting business owners and a social committee to plan the event with décor, food, and entertainment. I only needed to oversee some awesome volunteers. While driving to meet with the two teams, I asked the Lord how I should start off that meeting. Immediately a question came to mind that I should start with. As the meeting began, I asked all the volunteers if they remembered their wedding days. They all nodded yes. Then I asked if any of them had the experience of everything going right that day. They all shook their heads no. Next question, what was the purpose of that day, to have everything go right or to say, "I do?" They all agreed it was the latter. Then, I encouraged them to remember that point, not by focusing on what might go wrong but on the purpose of the event. All those women confided in me that the questions I asked diffused all their negative concerns and contentions with one another.

Only God knows the details we're unaware of and can give us counsel to successfully navigate life's mysteries. In the case of this event, wisdom's excellence brought needed solutions, diffused conflicting mindsets, and gave me the right words to say at the right time to bring clarity of purpose. The women responded so well to this God-given wisdom that they put on that gala without further complaint, enjoying the whole process.

Job proclaimed that the Almighty God is excellent in power, judgment, and moral uprightness (Job 37:23). God's counsel is excellent. His knowledge is excellent (Proverbs 22:20). His loving kindness is excellent (Psalm 36:7). His acts are great and excellent (Psalm 150:2). When we receive wisdom from above, our words become life-giving, and our spirits excellently reflect Jesus' dwelling within us (Proverbs 17:27).

The king of Babylon recognized that Daniel walked in the excellence of God's wisdom. Daniel's excellent spirit came from the wisdom he received from above. It was pure and innocent wisdom that was not self-seeking or manipulative. He truly desired to do good service to this king who had taken his people captive (Daniel 5:14). Because of that excellence of wisdom, Daniel was preferred above governors and princes (Daniel 6:3). This same wisdom is available to all of us who are God's children. All we need do is ask God for it. His wisdom illuminates a more excellent way to live that is far superior to the wisdom this natural world offers (1 Corinthians 12:31).

Wisdom, then, more perfectly reveals the person of Jesus to us. He gives us understanding and teaches us how to fear the Lord by filling us with bold confidence in Him as our knowledge of Him and His ways increases. We need to have an ear tuned to hear His voice whenever He speaks to us.

How about you? Have you asked the Lord for His wisdom? Have you paused long enough to hear Him? It may seem like an insignificant thing, such as my question to the gala committee members, but just asking those simple, off-topic questions created room for the Lord to do what only He could do to correct their attitudes and calm their frustrations. He will do it for you as well. Ask, hear or see, and then do. Then, stand back and watch the excellency of His wisdom unravel the hardship in front of you. Wisdom from above is superior in every way to the limitations of natural wisdom.

Does His wisdom sound too simple? Do it anyway. Do you feel His wisdom is too harsh? First, ask Him for merciful words to speak or a kind act to carry out; then say or do what He has spoken or shown you. You will find His wisdom to be excellent in value.

# THE EVIDENCE OF WISDOM

"But of Him you are in Christ Jesus, who became for us wisdom from God and righteousness and sanctification and redemption." –1 Corinthians 1:30 [NEW KING JAMES VERSION]

A week went by before the major called to inform me that the doctor had gone along with his recommendation. Jeremy would be honorably separated from the Marine Corps and sent home. The ordeal was over. Relief and gratitude sprung up in my heart!

Still, the enemy of our faith wasn't quite finished with his attack of confusion. We were awaiting the day of return, only to be put off another day, then another. Two days before Jeremy was to come home, he called and said, "Mom, pray that I am not delayed in coming home. There's been a bomb threat at the base preventing all departures. This hasn't ever happened before, Mom."

So, we prayed and rejoiced through this last resistance of the enemy. Honestly, I found myself laughing in the face of this last threat of failure. No weapon designed to hinder the Lord's purposes would be successful.

Indeed, our son came home. He had been honorably discharged. What a day of relief, rejoicing, and praise to our King Jesus. What a tremendous time of growth in our faith in God we experienced! His wisdom gave strength, counsel, and understanding. He was always the one in ultimate control of the whole situation.

With the utmost confidence, I can say that the Lord God is faithful. He was and is my stronghold in the day of trouble (Nahum 1:7). He runs quickly to the aid of those who put their trust in Him. He's not afraid of our bouts with doubts. He's the healer of those doubts. He brings stability to our hearts and gives our spirits cause to rejoice. He upholds us in the day of trouble with His strong right arm. Let His name be magnified forever and ever! Throughout this journey, I learned to fear the Lord. My aim was to respectfully revere Him in all areas of my life. This awesome fear, this respectful reverence, became the evidence that His wisdom guided my life and will continue to do so. It is important to walk humbly before Him and to rightly love ourselves and others. This attitude of the soul brings awareness to the river of life shooting up like a fountain of refreshment. Our words become enriched with gracious kindness. When wisdom resides in our hearts, we learn to walk circumspectly. That simply means we carefully pay attention to our circumstances, noting the possible consequences of each course of action we could take. Then, we wisely choose the least harmful path.

Being wise in justice also helps you take note of moral and legal boundaries. Wise judgment rules one's decisions, preventing faulty opinions of judgment. Discernment will enable you to act with a humble heart. From this humility, you will reap the rewards of God's faithfulness—He will guide, lead, and deliver you from all harm. Wisdom guards our equity with God's truth. Knowledge of God leads you into His wisdom, encouraging you to do what pleases Him. It will point you to rightly applying your understanding of God and His ways. Others may not agree with or understand your choices at the time, but they will certainly see the results and be amazed at the excellence of His wisdom.

Receiving God's wisdom also gives us strategies from heaven, as I experienced. Wisdom provides you with a supernatural ability to observe and experience the fulfillment of God's purposes in your life while side-stepping every perverse and false way.

What should we look for as evidence that wisdom functions in our lives? Scripture has much to reveal about that. It really begins by simply asking the Lord out of a deep, respectful reverence for Him. When you ask the Lord for His wisdom, act on what He has said. Do or say what He has told you to do or say. His wisdom displays His wondrous solutions. Proverbs 9:10 declares that the fear of the Lord is the beginning of wisdom, and the knowledge of the Holy One is understanding. This verse defines "beginning" as the first fruit, or the first evidence, of wisdom appearing in our lives. This foundational element in a believer's life is crucial in wisdom's development. Wisdom, or the quality of being wise, knowledgeable, and skillful, generates a capacity to use knowledge correctly. Job 28:28 [NKJV] puts it this way— "The fear of the Lord, that is wisdom, and to depart from evil is understanding." Understanding combined with discernment helps us know what the Lord would have us do or speak and discern what is right from wrong.

When the Levites taught the scriptures throughout the cities of Judah, not only did God's own people turn away from unrighteousness but the fear of the Lord fell on all the kingdoms around Judah (2 Chronicles 17:9-10). Why? Because there was a difference in the way they lived their lives that was supernatural yet practical, observable, and powerfully safe. Living by the truth of scripture brought that kingdom into godly wisdom from above. The truth in God's wisdom will do the same for you.

That type of lifestyle honors the Lord. It is evidenced by a whole-hearted obedience of His commands (Psalm 86:11). Wisdom enables you to serve the Lord in sincerity and truth (Joshua 24:14). You will find that your conversations continually tell of God's goodness, where you no longer speak or behave like the world around you (Psalm 34:11, 66:16; Deuteronomy 6:5-7). A lifestyle of wisdom receives a response from God—His watchful eye is ever upon us to deliver and protect our souls (Psalm 33:18-19). He gladly shares His secrets with us. He explains the eternal covenant He has made with us (Psalm 25:12). Therefore, we grab hold of His covenant with the understanding of wisdom, fully confident in His faithfulness to come to our aid in times of trouble. He is our strong confidence, our place of refuge, and a fountain of life to our souls (Proverbs 14:26-27). The deep satisfaction of heart, soul, and mind that others long for is yours just by walking in God's wisdom daily (Proverbs 19:23).

The understanding that comes with godly wisdom often opens the door to speaking words of wise counsel to others. You may find yourself being sought out to give counsel to those struggling with con-fusion. Be bold. Speak the word the Lord gives you. Words of life easily flow out of the mouths of those who love God's wisdom because they ask for it frequently. Speaking grace-filled, wise words increases your influence of good to those around you (Proverbs 4:7-10). Wisdom may even promote you to a reputation of honor among your friends and colleagues. How? When you stop to hear words from the Lord, receive them, then act on them. This is evidence that you are giving the Lord His rightful place as your wise counselor. His counsel will bring His purposes into your life as well as the lives of those you influence.

Wisdom will prolong your days by leading you into the Lord's steps (Proverbs 4:10-12). Perhaps this means saying "no" to what you would normally involve yourself in by saying "yes" to what the Lord is whispering to your heart. In fact, these verses in Proverbs state that "the years of your life will be many" when we walk in the wisdom of God's ways (Proverbs 4:10).

Jeremy certainly is experiencing this truth in the fact that the Lord prevented his death from heat stroke, then redirected his steps away from military training. Walking in wisdom allows the Lord to direct your steps away from harm—away from His purpose for you. His word of wisdom will fill you with confidence even when feeling pressured by your circumstances, just like Jeremy experienced. You, too, can run swiftly into obedient faith without stumbling. By letting scripture instruct you, you can confidently navigate obstacles in your life, and can rest assured that the Lord, in His infinite wisdom, will protect and guard your life.

As a parent, I chose to lead my son into God's wisdom throughout our journey together. All leaders need wisdom as they lead, regardless of their sphere of influence. You could be responsible for a platoon, a business, or a child, but you'll need wise understanding if you want to lead them well. The excellence of wisdom is mandatory for carrying out your responsibilities in a way that honors the Lord. It will also honor those you are leading. If you are leading anyone, make sure to ask the Lord for wisdom. He will give it to you just like He did for me as Vice President of the American Women's Club when I was putting together the gala.

His wisdom simplifies our conflicts, distresses, and hardships. He will reveal His purpose, strategy, and divine plan so you can lead well (Proverbs 8:12, 14-16). His wisdom will incorporate His justice balanced with His mercy. Those you lead will find themselves looking to you as a mentor in wisdom.

Godly wisdom will be evident in your attitude as it guards your heart from pride. Remember Daniel when he was called before the king? He was offered gifts of wealth and prestige for his skill in interpreting the king's dream. But the humility of his heart, produced by the wisdom of God, prevented Daniel from accepting payment for the interpretation. Wisdom is like that. It's a precious thing to be valued and stewarded well, not necessarily for monetary gain, but for the benefit of the one receiving it, just as we do when we receive it from the Lord.

When wisdom fills your life, you become aware of the Lord's protective hand surrounding you. Knowing He is with you to help you walk in His ways produces a pleasure deep within your soul. In times of uncertainty, His wisdom leads you straight into His supernatural peace (Proverbs 2:10). God's protective hand is a delivering hand. His wisdom will teach you how to sidestep harm, avoid unhealthy relationships, and refrain from dishonest or contrary conversations as He reveals His path to you.

Just think about the transformation in how you speak. Wisdom turns your thoughts and words from negatives into truths. Truth relieves anxieties and fears. Hence, your life is endowed with peace and safety. Even your dreams at night become peaceful rather than troubled (Proverbs 3:21-26). Why? Because wisdom becomes a refreshing stream of life to your soul, surrounding you with God's grace throughout the day and night.

Just as first-century believers walked in the fear of the Lord, providing them with comfort that built their faith, so can you (Acts 9:31). The same Holy Spirit who comforted them is ready to do the same for you. They shared that comfort in word and deed with others, bringing about a multiplication of believers into God's kingdom. This same wisdom that comforts, encourages, builds confident faith, and offers strategy from the Lord is available to you today. Wisdom from above is yours whenever you ask for it. Our gracious God will give you wisdom in abundance.

I will leave you with this encouragement from Proverbs 8:33-35. Don't just ask as you run out the door, but stop to listen to the Lord's voice, be it spoken to your inner self or through His scriptures. Listen attentively. Take time to write down what He has impressed upon you. His words will infuse you with the blessings of His powerful goodness just because you pause to ask, take time to hear, then act on it.

Do this daily, not just in times of distress. You'll find the Lord's favor when asking Him for wisdom. And you'll find great pleasure in the riches of His righteousness as you receive His wisdom (Proverbs 8:18). Ask and receive it daily from His heart and watch how His wisdom transforms your life into a rich testimony of His great goodness and love.

# ACKNOWLEDGMENTS

This book developed due to the many encouragements from a variety of people – family, friends, and ministers of the Gospel who told me, "The Lord has placed many books within you." Alongside those encouragements, the Holy Spirit prompted me to put pen to paper. Thank you, Jesus, for those promptings and for sending those ministers into my life at the right time.

I want to thank my husband, Chuck, for your continual support throughout this writing season. You have been my rock with your sense of humor to get me over the frustrations and the moments where I've wanted to quit. You have willingly invested our finances into this endeavor and your time to help me as needed when navigating computer programs. Your patience and encouragement have been invaluable.

Thank you, Jeremy, one of my three precious sons, for agreeing to allow me to share my side of your personal journey of growing your trust of the Lord Jesus through your own time of stress and confusion. You are a man of grace! And a treasure to my heart.

Thank you, Joshua, my artistically talented son who agreed to design this book's cover. You did an excellent job. I'm so proud of you! Also, your help with navigating and educating me on what programs would benefit me in getting this book to its finished end of being published has been invaluable.

A huge thank you to all my friends who have told me that you would read anything I write while looking forward to my first book – Karli Nash, Cheryl Sandifer, Toni Hart, Eva Joy, Melody Ochterbeck, Charles and Tera Saunders, and so many others. Your words of encouragement always came at the right time to help me keep on writing.

I especially give thanks to you, Mandy Reiszner, for your frequent encouragements, enthusiasm, and excitement towards me getting this book written so you can share it with your ministry team. Your encouragement helped me push through those times when I questioned whether or not to continue this writing process.

Thank you to my writing coach, Karen Pina, for challenging me to set a timeframe goal to get my rough draft done. Thank you, Matt Emmorey, for your coaching calls that encouraged me to keep going while providing me with advice on what next needed to be focused on.

A huge thank you to Carrie Turner, my wonderful editor, who went through my manuscript with expertise each period of editing required. Your skills have been invaluable. (You can find her at Carrie Turner Writing & Editing Services; https://www.carriebturner.com).

# ABOUT THE AUTHOR

Wanda Anderson has been a Bible teacher to many for the past fifty years as she and her husband have traveled internationally, living in both the Middle East and Germany for several years. With a Bachelor of Theology as well as a master's degree in biblical counseling, she has served in various capacities in the churches she's attended—always teaching whatever age needed her. She has taught the Scriptures in Bible college, ladies' groups, Sunday School, from the pulpit, and in a discipleship training school as both director and teacher alongside her husband. She and her husband led a house church for fourteen years in Texas. She has also traveled with various ministries both within the USA and internationally. She continues to teach and mentor others. Currently she enjoys traveling to see her three wonderful sons, and to love on her grandchildren. You can contact her at wandadelightsinthelord@gmail.com or visit her website delightsoftruth.com.

www.ingramcontent.com/pod-product-compliance
Lightning Source LLC
Chambersburg PA
CBHW061657120626
46550CB00003B/976